A THEOLOGICAL/EXEGETICAL
APPROACH TO GLOSSOLALIA

A THEOLOGICAL/EXEGETICAL APPROACH TO GLOSSOLALIA

WATSON E. MILLS

UNIVERSITY
PRESS OF
AMERICA

LANHAM • NEW YORK • LONDON

All University Press of America books are produced
on acid-free paper that exceeds
the minimum standards set
by the National Historical Publication and Records Commission.

UNIVERSITY
PRESS OF
AMERICA

For
the congregation
of the
Sharpsburg Baptist Church
Sharpsburg, Georgia
with
appreciation and gratitude

CONTENTS

PREFACE

I first became interested in the study of glossolalia when I was searching for a dissertation topic at Southern Baptist Theological Seminary in 1966. At that time I had had no first-hand knowledge of the phenomenon of speaking in tongues. I knew of its existence only from reading and class lectures. Like many of my colleagues, I had associated glossolalia with a "brand" of Christianity that seemed remote from and foreign to me.

As I began my study, I was surprised to discover that the convenient stereotypes I had inherited (and adopted) were not very workable. There were honest folk on both sides of this question who were genuinely struggling to find meaning in the faith.

Over the years I have continued to study this aspect of the Christian faith. Though I am not a practioner, I believe I can say I have come to be a part of a movement toward greater tolerance on the part of all those who are involved in these discussions.

This book is an attempt to get at what the scriptures say about the phenomenon of tongue speaking, and to evaluate that evidence from the standpoint of the larger arena of biblical theology.

I wish to express my appreciation to Ms. Irene Pace who prepared all drafts of this manuscript and to Ms. Sandra Keaton who assisted with the preparation of the bibliography.

Watson E. Mills
Macon, GA
1984

1

INTRODUCTION

In the midst of a charismatic revival which G. J. Sirks has appropriately characterized as "The Cinderella of Theology"[1] Christendom today finds herself facing new and pressing problems. Certainly a significant development during the last two decades has been the phenomenal rise of charismatic religion. One attendant feature of this "new wave" is glossolalia or "speaking in tongues." Twenty years ago it was described as one of the "fastest growing fads in U.S. Protestant churches."[2] Today no one would dismiss the phenomenon so lightly because the charismatic numbers have swelled dramatically cutting across virtually all denominational lines.

Reaction to the movement has been widely divergent. Early assessments were far from neutral. Some, for instance, dismissed tongues as "praying in gibberish,"[3] "fluent non-

---

[1]G. J. Sirks, "The Cinderella of Theology: The Doctrine of the Holy Spirit," *The Harvard Theological Review*, 50 (1957): 77-89.

[2]"Taming the Tongues," *Time*, 84 (July 10, 1964): 66.

[3]Ibid. Verbatim examples of glossolalia show a strong tendency towards alliteration and repetition. Cf. John P. Newport, "Speaking with Tongues," *Home Missions*, 36 (May 1965): 9.

sense,"[4] "heresy in embryo,"[5] and "esoteric self-indulgence."[6] One critic flatly summarized the matter this way: "God does not deal in trivialities, obscurities, and unintelligible gibberish."[7] These earlier unsympathetic estimates of the significance of glossolalia have given way to much greater levels of tolerance as the charismatic movement began to penetrate into wider segments of Christendom. As early as 1967 Wayne E. Oates concluded that to reject the phenomenon with "pejorative judgment" is "just as harsh and judgmental as if we reject the language of children because it is babbling and not understandable."[8]

Those who are involved in the experience of glossolalia often write about the phenomenon in an experiential, semi-apologetic manner. John L. Sherrill, for example, described the experience as a "most beautiful outpouring of vowels and consonants. . . ."[9] A Yale University student, focusing upon the excitement the experience brought to his life, likened it to "driving a nitroglycerine truck down a dirt road."[10] One glossolalist reportedly remarked: "I saw praying hands grab the

---

[4]Donovan Bess, " 'Speaking in Tongues'—the High Church Heresy," *Nation*, 197 (1962): 173.

[5]James A. Pike, "Pastoral Letter Regarding 'Speaking in Tongues,' " *Pastoral Psychology*, 15 (May 1964): 58.

[6]Everett W. Palmer, "Speaking in Tongues," *Christian Advocate*, 8 (October 22, 1964): 10.

[7]Stuart Bergsma, *Speaking With Tongues* (Baker Book House, 1965), p. 24.

[8]Wayne E. Oates, "A Socio-Psychological Study of Glossolalia," in *Glossolalia: Tongue Speaking in Biblical, Historical, and Psychological Perspective*, Frank Stagg, E. Glenn Hinson and Wayne E. Oates, editors (Abingdon Press, 1967), p. 77.

[9]John L. Sherill, *They Speak with Other Tongues* (Revell, 1964), p. 19.

[10]Quoted in Harald Bredesen, "Discovery at Yale," *Trinity*, 1 (Christmastide 1962-1963): 16.

Holy power of God in a most supernatural way. . . . I saw God's men and women, boys and girls, saturated in the flaming power of the Holy Spirit."[11]

The inescapable conclusion of these and other estimates of the phenomenon is the need for a fairly definitive and objective means whereby to evaluate the tongues phenomenon. The purpose of the present study is to set forth the theological relevance of glossolalia, if any, and to relate the experience of tongues[12] to the larger context of biblical theology.

In this volume the term "tongues" is a synonym for the term "glossolalia" which may be defined as: "a spontaneous utterance of uncomprehended and seemingly random speech sounds. The speech itself rises in an effortless flow, with the repetition and inflection characteristic of language in general."

New Testament theology is certainly the most important if not the most difficult of New Testament studies. One reason for this difficulty is that New Testament theology depends for its existence upon several other disciplines—textual, historical and literary criticisms—and these derive their significance as they bear upon New Testament theology. While it depends upon these disciplines, however, it is also bound to go beyond them. Ideally, New Testament theology is the "crowning discipline" that interprets and integrates the other branches of theological investigation.

The task of New Testament theology is exegetical rather than purely speculative or dogmatic; and it is exegetical in a double sense, i.e., it must understand the text historically as well as existentially. New Testament theology, as Krister Sten-

---

[11]Quoted in *Methodists and the Baptism of the Holy Spirit* (Full Gospel Business Men's Fellowship International, 1963), p. 22.

[12]While the term "tongue" has various connotations in the New Testament, the present work deals only with the theological significance of the technical usage of the term, i.e., as in "speaking in tongues," commonly referred to as *glossolalia*. The terms "speaking in tongues," "tongues," and "glossolalia" are herein synonymous.

dahl observed, must address itself to the problem of "what it [the text] *meant* and what it *means*" [italics added].[13]

The method employed here is that of "theological exegesis." The task of this endeavor is to relate the religious and theological content of the Bible, as it has been determined by historical exegesis, to the individual in his immediate situation. Moreover this "relational" activity must occur in an existential context sufficient to speak to the believer's needs. Therefore, if we are to assess the significance of glossolalia theologically for contemporary man, it is first necessary to clarify its significance for the New Testament writers. The method herein employed, however, is only *secondarily* that of "historical exegesis" and *primarily* that of "theological exegesis"; the former being concerned with the message in its *original setting*, the latter with the message as it has *contemporary relevance*. This is obviously, however, not a rigid distinction since the message for which the theological exegete searches and seeks to make relevant is always embodied in a given text; the theological exegete must labor hand-in-hand with the historical exegete.

The goal of "theological exegesis" is a biblical theology that is relevant both to the witness of scripture and in the contemporary situation; therefore, a "theological interpretation" of tongues includes both a comprehensive assessment of the biblical evidence as well as evaluation of its theological significance. For the biblical theologian "what it means" is paramount, even though this question presupposes a more basic one: "what it meant."

This writing is thus conceived to be an exercise in biblical theology; however, a corollary assumption is that the determination of the relevance of tongues for contemporary theology presupposes the question of *significance* of the phenomenon in the minds of the New Testament writers.

----

[13]Krister Stendahl, "Biblical Theology, Contemporary," *The Interpreter's Dictionary of the Bible*, George Arthur Buttrick, editor. 4 vols. (Abingdon Press, 1962), A-D:419.

2

GLOSSOLALIA IN THE JUDEO-CHRISTIAN TRADITION

One cannot but agree with James Montgomery, who noted that "every word has its own personality; a translation is but a mask."[1] So it is with the word "tongue," and this well may be precisely its glory. Its meanings are indeed many and diverse.

The purpose of this chapter is to set forth certain contextual considerations necessary to interpret tongues theologically in Acts and 1 Corinthians. After a general discussion of the biblical usages of the term "tongue," there follows a specific development of the technical usage as in "speaking in tongues." The relationship of glossolalia to ecstaticism in general and to the Old Testament in particular will be treated.

BIBLICAL USES OF THE TERM *TONGUE*

The word "tongue" (לָשׁוֹן, γλῶσσα) has several connotations in

---

[1]James A. Montgomery, "Hebrew *Hesed* and Greek *Charis*," *The Harvard Theological Review*, 32 (April 1959): 101.

biblical usage. Obviously, it is a part of the physical make-up of man.[2] Being an organ of speech, it represented the various languages and dialects of mankind; and men were held to be different "essentially" when they spoke a "foreign" language.[3] This difference appears to achieve the status of a threat in Jeremiah 5:15:

> Behold, I am bringing upon you a nation from afar, O house of Israel, says the Lord. It is an enduring nation, it is an ancient nation, a nation whose language you do not know, nor can you understand what they say.

Similarly, the term was a synonym for "people" (Rev. 5:9, 7:9, 10:11, 11:9, 13:7, 14:6) and "nation" (Isa. 66:18).

Speaking, however, is more than a verbal activity; rather, it is an expression of the totality of man, his presuppositions and values. Thus, frequently the tongue is an agent closely related to the heart.[4] Considerable emphasis is placed upon the sins of the tongue in the Jewish literature.[5] In the Old Testament these references occur largely in the Psalter, Job and Proverbs (Prov. 6:17, 10:31, 17:4, 21:23; Ps. 51:4, 56:4, 63:3). The ancient sage observed that "he who keeps his mouth and his tongue keeps himself out of trouble" (Prov. 21:23). Apparently, however, in at least some circles, it was felt that no one could ultimately escape the sins of the tongue, for the author

---

[2]Cf. Judges 7:5; Isaiah 41:17; Luke 16:24; Revelation 16:10. It appears that tongues were a favorite article of diet as in Oxyrhynchus Papyri I, 108 in Bernard P. Grenfell, et al., editors, *The Oxyrhynchus Papyri* (29 vols.; Horace Hart, 1898-1963), 1:175.

[3]Griechische Papyri IC, 9 in Ernst Korneman and Paul M. Meyer (eds.), *Griechische Papyri zu Giessen* (3 vols.; B. B. Tübner, 1910), 3:93.

[4]Psalm 45:1; Proverbs 10:28, 17:20. Cf. P. Dhorme, "L'emploi metaphorique des noms de parties du corps en hébren et en akkadian," *Revue Biblique*, 30 (1921): 536-37.

[5]Johannes Behm, "γλῶσσα," in *Theological Dictionary of the New Testament*, Gerhard Kittel, editor; trans. Geoffrey W. Bromiley (10 vols.; Eerdmans, 1964-1976), 1:721.

of Sirach asks, "Who has never sinned with his tongue?" (Sir. 19:16b). The ancients believed that the tongue possessed every potentiality for good and for evil. In the New Testament this awareness of the infinite possibilities of the tongue is apparent in James. Here the writer uses as an analogy the rudder of a ship (James 3:4) and the bit in the mouth of a horse (James 3:3). The ethical context from which the epistle arose gives expression to that which lies just beneath the surface in much of the biblical material. Since the tongue reveals what is in the heart, the use of the tongue has moral implications. The psalmist suggests that one keep his "tongue from evil" and his "lips from speaking deceit" (Ps. 34:13).

Also, the Greek γλῶσσα has a magical significance that Adolf Deissmann has documented at length.[6] Mark 7:35,[7] he maintains, represents not only a figurative usage of the term, but it has also definite reference to being "bound of the tongue."[8] Richard Wünsch has published a series of tablets that contain references to "binding." Over thirty of these speak of binding or cursing "the tongue."[9]

---

[6] Adolf Deissmann, *Light From the Ancient East*, trans. Lionel R. M. Strachan (Hodder and Stoughton, 1910), pp. 304-10.

[7] The text of Mark 7:35 reads: "And his ears were opened, his tongue was released, and he spoke plainly." For a discussion of demonic possession in classical antiquity and early Christian times see T. K. Oesterreich, *Possession: Demonical and Other* (Richard R. Smith, 1930), pp. 155-67.

[8] Deissmann, op. cit., p. 306, notes that "running throughout all antiquity we find the idea that a man can be 'bound' or 'fettered' by demonic influences." Mark Lidaharski, *Ephemeris für semitische Epigraphik* (3 vols.; J. Ricker, 1902-1915), 1:31, documents this concept in Greek, Syrian, Hebrew, Mandaean and Indian magic spells.

[9] Richard Wünsch, *Corpus Inscriptionum Atticarum*. Cf. London Papyri 1, 121 in F. G. Kenyon and H. I. Bell, editors, *Greek Papyri in the British Museum* (5 vols.; Oxford University Press, 1893-1917), 1:114; Willhelm Dittenberger, *Sylloge Inscriptionum Graecarum* (3 vols.; 2nd. ed.; A. S. Hiraelium, 1888-1901), 2:671-72.

No usage of the term "tongue," however, presents more difficulty to the interpreter than its technical usage in the phrase λαλεῖν (ἐν) γλώσσῃ (γλώσσαις),[10] usually translated "speaking in tongues" or "glossolalia."[11] This phenomenon is referred to in 1 Corinthians 12-14 and in Acts 2:3ff., 10:46 and 19:6. It appears to describe a form of spiritually affected speaking which is of particular value to the individual. A striking phenomenon of primitive Christianity, glossolalia issues "from Christians who, in a state of *ecstasy*," believe "themselves to be possessed by the spirit"[12] [italics added]. Ecstaticism may be defined as:

> those religious phenomena in which the devotee is given to such conditions known to psychologists as trances, hypnotic states, or extreme euphoria, followed or accompanied by external behavior such as dancing, shouting, whirling, jerking, prostration, and speaking with tongues, or glossolalia.

Because of the implicit connection of glossolalia with ecstatic phenomena in general, a survey of the development of ecsta-

---

[10]The expression is taken to mean about the same thing as λαλεῖν γλώσσαις καιναῖς in Mark 16:17 and ἑτέραις γλώσσαις in Acts 2:4. For further discussion see Friedrich Blass and A. Debrunner, *A Greek Grammar of the New Testament and Other Early Christian Literature*, trans. Robert W. Funk (rev. ed.; University of Chicago Press, 1961), p. 254: "In similar narrative in Acts (10:46, 19:6) ἑτέραις has only weak versional support, and is always omitted by Paul."

[11]Just how the term γλῶσσα came to be a technical term for this rather ecstatic mode of expression is not clear. Behm, op. cit., p. 726, concludes that "it . . . seems most likely that the word γλῶσσα has here the sense of language . . . namely, the 'language of the Spirit.' " Cf. Eddison Mosiman, *Das Zungenreden geschichtlich und psychologisch untersucht* (J. C. B. Mohr, 1911), p. 35, who notes that the term was so used for "a peculiar language."

[12]Elias Andrews, "Tongues, Gift of," *The Interpreter's Dictionary of the Bible*, George Arthur Buttrick, editor (4 vols.; Abingdon Press, 1962), R-Z:671.

ticism and its relationship to the Old Testament prophets follows.

ECSTATICISM

The interpretation of the Christian experience of glossolalia would be a great deal simpler if any relatively contemporary non-Christian examples of similar phenomena could be gleaned from the extant literature for comparison. This section proposes to investigate this possibility.[13] The discovery of similar phenomena does not establish any organic or psychic relationship to the Christian gift of tongues. Rather, it would indicate that such phenomena attest to the general tendency on the part of mankind to seek the aid of his god in varying degrees of persistence and intensity. A common way to objectify the attainment of this quest was to break forth in frenzied or ecstatic speech.

Ecstaticism Outside the Old Testament

The Judeo-Christian tradition is not entirely responsible for the origin and perpetuation of ecstaticism. Historical evidence indicates that ecstaticism was much more a universal phenomenon. It has been suggested that "the Christian tradition of speaking-in-tongues probably had its roots in the ancient religions of Asia Minor."[14] The earliest report of an experience is found in the report of Wenamon, an Egyptian who journeyed through Palestine and Phoenicia about 1117 B.C. While in Byblos he wrote the following account:

> Now when he sacrificed to his gods, the god seized one of his noble youths, making him frenzied, so that he said: 'Bring

---

[13]For a dated but comprehensive bibliography on ecstaticism see Mosiman, op. cit., p. ix.

[14]Carlyle L. May, "A Survey of Glossolalia and Related Phenomena in Non-Christian Religions," *American Anthropologist*, 58 (February 1956): 75.

> [the god] hither! Bring the messenger of Amon who hath him.
> Send him, and let him go.'

> Now, while the frenzied [youth] continued in frenzy dur-
> ing this night, I found a ship bound for Egypt, and I loaded all
> my belongings into it. I waited for the darkness, saying:
> 'When it descends I will embark the god also, in order that no
> other eye may see him.'[15]

The report indicates that Zakar-Baal deferred to this frenzied
youth, and heeded what he had to say. The conclusion is that
such ecstatic or frenzied utterances were thought to be of divine origin.

Several factors emerge from the report which are significant: (1) the report indicates that the youth is possessed by a
god; (2) since he is a devout worshipper of Amon, the frenzied
speech appears to be viewed as a religious phenomenon; (3)
his ecstatic speech contained some words coherently understandable; (4) Wenamon evidently regards the youth as wor-
thy of protection and respect.

About the end of the second millenium before Christ,
there occurred a revival of the worship of Dionysus. This
movement swept rapidly over Greece and Syria-Palestine. The
devotees experienced a kind of religious rapture or ecstasy
"whose closest analogy is furnished by physical
intoxication."[16]

> The truth is that sheer physical intoxication from the drinking
> of wine was the essence of Dionysian religion. In the service
> of the god the Bacchanals drank wine until they were intoxi-

---

[15]"The Frenzied Youth" in the *Report of Wenamon* cited in James
Henry Breasted, *Ancient Records of Egypt* (5 vols.; University of Chicago Press, 1906), 4:278. The inscription may also be found in James
B. Pritchard, *Ancient Near Eastern Texts* (Princeton University Press,
1950), pp. 25-29.

[16]Friedrich Nietzsche, *The Birth of Tragedy*, trans. Francis Golffing
(Doubleday Anchor Books, 1956), p. 22.

cated. . . . The wine they drank was for them potent with divine power—it was the god himself, and the very quintessence of divine life was resident in the juice of the grape. . . . Their enthusiasm was quite literally a matter of having the god within themselves, of being full of and completely possessed by the god.[17]

The Dionysiac cult may be likened to " 'revival meetings'— and these of a very emotional and exciting sort."[18] The ecstaticism of the cult is apparent in the following description:

The dances in honor of Dionysus were usually held at night time by torchlight and were preceded by fasting. They were accompanied by the weird music of wind instruments and the clashing of tambourines. Mingled with this strange music were the shouts of the Bacchanals themselves as they waved their torches in the darkness, thus giving to the scene an unearthly light. The dances were wild and irregular and were characterized by a tossing of the head and a violent, whirling bodily motion. Thus by the very movements of the dance a physical frenzy was quickly induced, quite as the 'dancing dervishes' of Mohammedanism lose control of themselves in the delirium of their ritual.[19]

Euripides, in the *Bacchae*, describes how these Dionysiac worshippers longed for this ecstatic experience.

Ah, shall my white feet in the dances gleam
The livelong night again? Ah, shall I there

---

[17]Harold R. Willoughby, *Pagan Regeneration: A Study of Mystery Initiations in the Graeco-Roman World* (University of Chicago Press, 1929), p. 74-75.

[18]James B. Pratt, *The Religious Consciousness* (Macmillan and Company, 1937), p. 167.

[19]Willoughby, op.cit., p. 79.

Float through the Bacchanal's ecstatic dream,
Tossing my neck in the dewy air?[20]

At this point, Israelite ecstaticism is somewhat akin to the frenzy of the Dionysiac worshippers. "The legendary Bacchantic irruption into Greece," writes W. F. Albright, "of which Euripides wrote so eloquently, and the prophetic movement in Israel may have a common historical source."[21] It is sociologically and psychologically credible that the ecstaticism of the early Yahwists is a part of the same general religious atmosphere that the Dionysus worshippers were part of, although it is plainly evident that Yahwistic ecstaticism followed a very different line of development after the eleventh century B.C. Nonetheless, it is likely that the Yahwistic movement arose partly out of reaction against ecstaticism.[22]

Ecstaticism in the Old Testament

The trail of historical appearances of ecstaticism leads directly to the milieu out of which the Old Testament literature arose. The first reference in the Old Testament material to the ecstatic is found in Numbers 11:24-29. Here is a clear picture of a frenzied, involuntary utterance. The occasion was the selection of the seventy elders who were to assist Moses in leadership responsibilities. These elders demonstrated ecstaticism (Num. 11:26) as did Moses (Num. 11:17), Miriam (Num. 12:1,

---

[20]Euripides, *Bacchae*, 862-65 in Whitney J. Oates and Eugene O'Neill (eds.), *The Complete Greek Drama* (2 vols.; Random House, 1938), 2:260.

[21]Albright, op. cit., p. 305. Cf. also E. R. Dodds, "Maenadism in the Bacchae," *The Harvard Theological Review*, 33 (July 1940): 155-76.

[22]The Mari Texts have been helpful in understanding the function of the mantic prophet who passed on to high state officials communications which he had received in dreams. Cf. A. Lods, "Une tablette inodite de Mari, interessante pour l'histoire ancienne du prophetisme semitique," *Studies in Old Testament Prophecy*, H. H. Rowley, editor (T. & T. Clark, 1950), pp. 130ff.

12:2) and Aaron (Num. 12:1). It appears that this phenomenon caused much chagrin for Joshua (Num. 11:28) and some anxiety for at least one young man (Num. 11:27). The account indicates that the seventy became frenzied on this occasion *only*. Eldad and Medad, who were left behind at the camp, "prophesied." Moses recognized the validity of the phenomenon and suggested that others seek the same experience. The entire episode is in no wise regarded as a psychopathic situation. On the contrary, the experience is set in a religious context and is given religious significance.

The earliest detailed examples of ecstaticism in the Hebraic tradition are to be found among the prophets. Originally the prophets went about in bands which formed a kind of separate society within society. In keeping with this societal status, the prophets were commonly designated "sons of prophets" (2 Kings 2:3, 2:5, 2:6, 2:15; Amos 2:11, 7:14) by subsequent generations. Von Rad sees no reason to doubt the existence of bands of ecstatic prophets[23] as late as the time of David,[24] quite possibly living together in communal dwellings.[25] These roving bands were considered to be inspired by the Spirit. A central passage for ascertaining the nature of this inspiration is found in 1 Samuel 10:5b-6:

> . . . you will meet a band of prophets coming down from the high place with harp, tambourine, flute, and lyre before

---

[23]Some scholars think that the term נָוִית is a designation for the dwelling place of these prophets. Cf. 1 Samuel 19:18ff, 19:22ff, 20:1. See Johannes Pedersen, *Israel, Its Life and Culture* (4 vols.; Oxford University Press, 1947), 3-4:109, 678.

[24]von Rad, op. cit., p. 10. Cf. Amos 7:14. Note also that Alfred Guillaume, *Prophecy and Divination Among the Hebrews and Other Semites* (Hodder and Stoughton, 1938), pp. 144-45, claims that "in 853 B.C. four hundred prophets raved in ecstasy before the gate of Samaria."

[25]Cf. Walther Eichrodt, *Theology of the Old Testament*, trans. J. A. Baker (2 vols.; Westminster Press, 1961), 1:315.

> them, prophesying. Then the spirit of the Lord will come
> mightily upon you, and you shall prophesy with them and be
> turned into another man.

While it appears that Saul's behavior is spontaneous, the band
of prophets has employed a certain "technique for bringing on
the ecstatic condition."[26] The resultant ecstasy is highly con-
tagious, and Saul appears to be caught up in it. Music was
commonly used to induce this ecstasy.[27] Also, among the earlier prophets as in the case of the Baal prophets, various drugs
and wines may have been employed.[28]

The term *nabi* itself is derived from the condition of ecstatic
frenzy into which the subject passes; hence, the term denotes
a "raving condition" or one who is "peculiarly susceptible to
ecstatic excitement."[29] This interpretation suits the meaning of
the word exactly. The prophet was a man who felt himself
called by God for a special mission. His will was subordinated
to the will of God. The prophet was thus a kind of charismatic
spiritual leader.[30]

Some scholars maintain that ecstatic forms of prophecy
were native to Canaanite rather than Hebrew culture, and that
Canaanite religion may have been the medium through which

---

[26]Francis J. McConnell, *The Prophetic Ministry* (Abingdon Press,
1930), p. 86. For further discussion of the relationship of glossolalia
to the prophets see Émile Lombard, *De la Glossolalie chez les premiers
Chrétiens* (Bridel, 1910), pp. 189ff.

[27]1 Samuel 10:5 refers to a "psaltry and a timbrel, and a pipe, and
a harp." Cf. 2 Kings 3:15.

[28]Theodore H. Robinson, *Prophecy and the Prophets* (Gerald Duckworth and Company, 1950), p. 32.

[29]Harold Knight, *The Hebrew Prophetic Consciousness* (Lutterworth
Press, 1947), p. 23. Cf. Guillaume, op. cit., pp. 112ff.

[30]Albright, op. cit., p. 303.

ecstaticism first migrated into Israelite religion.[31] Various "pagan" parallels are cited,[32] and generally it is assumed that the Hebrew people first encountered the phenomenon at the time of the conquest and during the settlement of Canaan.[33] On the other hand, some of the earlier literary materials refer to similar phenomena in Israel prior to the time of the conquest.[34] Moreover, succeeding generations became so suspicious of the ecstatic form of prophecy that the prophet was considered to be "mad," and the prophet of the eighth century did not hesitate to say so.[35] If the influence of the later prophetic movement is to be seen in the Numbers account of Eldad and Medad, it is most likely the writing into it of the distrust of ecstatic prophecy of that later time and not in the account of the prophecy itself. Even though ecstatic experiences and states in prophecy can be more fully documented in extra-canonical literature,[36] it does not necessarily follow that no comparable phenomena existed in pre-conquest Israel.

It is also necessary to distinguish between the *kind* of prophetic consciousness among the Israelites and their pagan neighbors. According to Canaanite interpretation the prophet was seized by the god, whose spokesman he was, so that the prophet became identified with that god.[37] This deification of

---

[31]Gerhard von Rad, *Old Testament Theology*, trans. D. M. G. Stalker (2 vols.; Oliver and Boyd, 1965), 1:8.

[32]Hughel Fosbroke, "The Prophetic Literature," *The Interpreter's Bible*, George Arthur Buttrick, editor (12 vols.; Abingdon Press, 1953), 1:202.

[33]Robinson, op. cit., p. 33.

[34]Cf. Numbers 11:25-29. Those who advocate this position interpret all references to prophecy prior to the conquest as being a revision of an earlier history carried out under the influence of a later prophetic movement.

[35]Hosea 9:7; Jeremiah 29:26. Cf. 2 Kings 9:11.

[36]Guillaume, op. cit., p. 111.

[37]Knight, loc. cit.

the human was assuredly most repugnant to the Hebrews, who resolutely insisted upon the vast distance which existed between God and his prophet.[38]

External patterns of behavior, such as incoherent speech, insensibility to pain, wild leaping and contortions, and abnormal expressions,[39] were manifested in the ecstasy of both the Hebrew prophets and those of the Canaanites. It would have been easy, therefore, for the two to merge into a kind of syncretistic form in subsequent generations; and such was probably the case.

> The Hebrew prophet cannot wholly escape the influence of the ecstatic phenomena with which he is confronted in Palestine, but he imparts to these unusual psychic states a new significance by interpreting them in accordance with the implicates of his own special psychology and theology.[40]

In light of this interpretation there develops a reaction of true prophetic enthusiasm among the Hebrews against the mystical-ecstatic forms of Canaanite culture; however, there is not a resulting, rigid distinction between the "cultic" and the "canonical" prophets. On the contrary, there were definitely ec-

---

[38]Furthermore, the prophetic inspiration of the Hebrews is different from that of the Canaanites and various other pagan types since the condition of the Hebrew prophet is not such that the "soul" departs temporarily from the body, as in Greek thought. Cf. Pedersen, op. cit., 1-11, 99-181 and Aubrey R. Johnson, *The Vitality of the Individual in the Thought of Ancient Israel* (University of Wales Press, 1949), pp. 52, 83. H. Wheeler Robinson, *Inspiration and Revelation in the Old Testament* (Clarendon Press, 1946), p. 180, shows how the typical Hebrew concept of inspiration was that of divine energy (רוּחַ) invading the soul (נֶפֶשׁ) of the prophet.

[39]Robinson, *Prophecy and the Prophets*, pp. 30-31.

[40]Knight, op. cit., p. 53.

static features among the writing prophets;[41] the difference lay in the fact that there was a continuous, gradual but definite, development away from ecstatic forms of prophecy toward the more ordered form of discourse.[42] By the time of the writing prophets there was evidently an intense dislike for the older form of spirit manifestation in prophecy which allowed for little, if any, intelligible communication.[43]

Also, there was a reaction against the use of artificial means by which one might appropriate spirit possession unto himself. The Hebraic belief was that the Spirit seized the prophet without warning and through no exercise of his energies. Consistent with this belief was the rejection of the magical manipulation of pagan holy men. Balaam was an exact type of the Mesopotamian diviner.[44] As such, his method was that of magic; and he fancied himself able to manipulate the powers of nature, and consequently of God, to such a degree that he could bring a curse upon his opponents.

---

[41]For example, Ezekiel's psychic transports (Ezek. 3:14, 11:5, 11:13, 37:1-10); Jeremiah's emotional outbursts (Jer. 4:19, 8:18-9:1, 10:19-20); Isaiah's vision in the temple (Is. 6:1-13); and Isaiah's mention of prophetic babblings (Is. 28:10-13). John Skinner, *Prophecy and Religion* (Harvard University Press, 1922), p. 4, n. 1.

[42]Robinson, *Inspiration and Revelation in the Old Testament*, p. 175.

[43]This may explain why the classical prophets made only peripheral use of the term to explain their own inspiration. Ibid., p. 179. Guillaume, op. cit., pp. 133-39, points out that these divine speakers are still referred to as *nebi'im* which suggests that there is no necessary connection between the term and the experience of ecstasy as often claimed.

[44]Numbers 22-24. Robert H. Pfeiffer, *Introduction to the Old Testament* (Harper and Brothers, 1941), pp. 277, 279, dates all oracles between 950 and 750 B.C. The date need not affect the fidelity of the report, so that one may hold that Balaam, himself, is the turning point, and not the story-teller.

In Balaam the transition from the heathen Kahin to the heathen prophet has already begun. The old order of ecstasy, of uncontrollable excitement, fading away into the trance of exhaustion, the search for omens, and the snatching at chance utterance, are all clearly marked in his prophetic poetry; but reliance on these things is completely subordinated to his personal conviction that God has spoken, and will speak, to the heart of His obedient servant. Already, on the behalf of prophecy, Balaam has repudiated divination, necromancy, and the casting of lots; though he still allows a certain importance to divination from objects seen in an ominous relation it is a significance related to, and controlled by, the will of God as it is revealed to him; and thus the omen is the confirmation of truth already perceived.[45]

The revolt against past superstitions which Balaam epitomized resulted in the rejection and repudiation of magic and all unethical practices in religion. Gradually, through the sheer moral force and righteous living of these great prophets, the ecstatic manifestation of possession of the deity was replaced by more moral concepts of the divine indwelling of the Spirit. That is to say, ecstasy was no longer held to be *just* fanatic behavior; on the contrary, the objective "proof" of possession issued forth in a state of spiritual exaltation for the persuasive communication of the message.[46] Gradually this brought about the very evidence and continuous resistance of the latter prophets to all abnormal demonstrations of spirit possession. Hosea said that "the prophet is a fool, the man of the spirit is mad" (Hosea 9:7), while Jeremiah writes in 29:26:

The Lord has made you priest instead of Jehoiáda the priest, to have charge in the house of the Lord over every madman who prophesies, to put him in stocks and a collar.

Developing, then, is a higher standard by which to evaluate

---

[45]Guillaume, op. cit., pp. 138-39.

[46]This distinction was not rigid, since there are examples of ecstaticism among the writing prophets.

spirit possession—no longer are ecstatic manifestations the sole criterion.

Ecstaticism in the Greek Period

The prophetic emphasis upon righteous living and moral obligations and responsibilities, greatly influenced the total Jewish attitude toward the appearance of the more superficial manifestations of spirit possession, and especially that of frenzied speech. In the later days of writing the books of the Old Testament, there was a growing sense of suspicion concerning the spiritual validity of ecstaticism (Zech. 13:3, 6; Ps. 74:9). As a consequence there is a scarcity of references to the phenomenon of ecstaticism during this period. Nevertheless, 2 Esdras affords one example of frenzied speech. In the account of Ezra's ecstaticism, the text reads:

> Then I opened my mouth, and behold, a full cup was offered to me; it was full of something like water, but its color was like fire, and I took it and drank; and when I had drunk it, my heart poured forth understanding, and wisdom increased in my breast, for my spirit retained its memory; and my mouth was opened, and was no longer closed.[47]

Turning to the Greek literature, there are three separate instances in which Plato reveals his knowledge of ecstatic speech. In *Phaedrus*[48] Plato discusses the question of "madness." He does this in terms of prophecy, inspiration, poetry and love. In discussing madness as prophecy, Plato alludes to the prophetess at Delphi, the priestess at Dodona, and Sibyl,

---

[47]2 Esdras 14:39-41 in *The Apocrypha of the Old Testament*, p. 49. Note the conflicting report regarding ecstatic speech in 1 Maccabees 4:46 in ibid., p. 198, which indicates that there was an absence of such ecstatic prophets who could instruct the people in religious matters.

[48]Plato, *Phaedrus*, 224 in R. G. Bury (trans.), Rohde, *Psyche* (Harcourt, Brace and Company, 1925), p. 471, for a discussion of the ecstatic in Plato.

all of whom, he thinks, have conferred great benefits upon Hellas through their ecstatic speaking when out of their senses, but when not, little or none. In connection with inspiration as madness, he refers to certain families where madness has entered with holy prayers, rites, and by inspired utterances. For Plato, the contemporary poets were much akin to the prophets and priestesses; they created their literary compositions during ecstatic trances and from ecstatic utterances. In Plato's discussion there seems to be a link between ecstatic speech and religious significance. Too, it should be noted that Plato himself regarded the persons so gifted as of more value than the normal, sane persons.[49]

In the *Ion*[50] Plato further describes the poets when he likens them unto the Corybantian revelers who became ecstatic both in action and in utterance. He likewise compared them with the Bacchic maidens of the Dionysian cult.

Again, in *Timaeus*[51] he sought to draw a distinction between the diviner and the true prophet. The diviner was pictured as similar to ecstatic persons—demented, unable to evaluate the visions which he sees or the words which he utters. In describing these diviners Plato ascribed to them certain features similar to those of glossolalists: their speech being due to spirit possession; their being unable to discern what they said while in a given ecstatic need; their state being unconscious. Plato recognized that many people had identified these diviners with the prophets of his own time, and so he was determined to draw a valid distinction. It is strangely similar to that distinction between prophets and glossolalists drawn by Saint Paul in 1 Corinthians 14.

----

[49]Cf. Ira J. Martin, *Glossolalia in the Apostolic Church: A Survey of Tongues Speech* (Berea College Press, 1940), pp. 77-78.

[50]Plato, *Ion*, 533-534 in Bury, op. cit., 3:421ff.

[51]Plato, *Timaeus*, 71-72 in Bury, op. cit., 7:287ff.

A final example of frenzied speech may be found in the *Aeneid*.[52] Virgil here refers to the Sibylline priestess on the isle of Delos. She is pictured as attaining her ecstatic speech in a haunted cave. After the priestess was "unified" with the god Apollo, she began to speak ecstatically. At times this speech was intelligible, and at others it was less coherent. The religious context and connotation of the story are apparent.

These accounts from the Greek period indicate the presence of this frenzied, inarticulate speech in the Graeco-Roman world. It appears that in at least some cases these practices are connected with religion and were given a religious interpretation and significance.

Ecstaticism in the First Century

Contrary to many modern writers,[53] the case is not so easily made for the existence of parallels to glossolalia among the religions of the first century. The sources dating from the first and second centuries of the Christian era, e.g., Strabo, Plutarch, Pausanias and Philo, indicate that the "oracles" *may* have been an intelligible, though difficult, language.[54] The or-

---

[52]Virgil, *Aeneid*, 259-260 in H. Rushton Fairclough (trans.), *Virgil*. "The Loeb Classical Library" (2 vols.; William Heinemann, 1922), 1:513.

[53]Cf. Clarence T. Craig, "Exegesis: The First Epistle to the Corinthians," *The Interpreter's Bible*, George Arthur Buttrick, editor (12 vols.; Abingdon Press, 1953), 10:146; Andrews, op. cit., p. 671; Behm, op. cit., p. 719ff; James Moffatt, *First Corinthians* (Harper and Brothers, 1933), pp. 207-208; Jean Héring, *The First Epistle of Saint Paul to the Corinthians*, trans. A. W. Heathcote and P. J. Allcock (Epworth Press, 1962), p. 128; Maurice Barnett, *The Living Flame* (Epworth Press, 1953), pp. 79-112.

[54]Plutarch describes the priestess as one who gave her message in "sweetness and embellishment . . . in verse of a grandiloquent and formal style with verbal metaphors and with a flute to accompany its delivery." Cf. Plutarch, *The Oracles at Delphi No Longer Given in Verse*, 22 in Frank Cole Babbitt (trans.), *Plutarch's Moralia*. "The

acle at Delphi was the most famous in the ancient world,[55] and several scholars declare that she uttered her prophecies in an ecstatic frenzy.

Strabo indicates that the Pythia at Delphi received the "breath" (πνεῦμα) that inspired a "divine frenzy" (ἐνθουσιαστικόν) and then uttered oracles in both verse and prose.[56] In addition, Plutarch refers to the emotional frenzy of the mystery religions. He quotes Herodotus regarding the rites of these groups: "Frenzy and shouting of throngs in excitement with tumultuous tossing of heads in the air."[57] Strabo gives an account of the whirling of cymbals and clanging of castanets that were used in the worship of Dionysus, Cybele, and others.[58] He also describes the shouts of "ev-ah" and the stamping of feet that produced a religious frenzy.[59]

Women usually played the ecstatic part in Hellenistic religion,[60] though Pausanias indicates that men once prophesied

---

Loeb Classical Library" (10 vols.; William Heinemann, 1944-1949), 5:321. He also mentioned the priestesses who gave response in prose, some having "an easy fluency and a bent towards composing poetry." Cf. Plutarch, op. cit., 23 in Babbitt, loc. cit. He said of the contemporary oracles that they "give nearly all their communications in brief, simple, and straight-forward language." Cf. Plutarch, op. cit., 29 in Babbitt, op. cit., 5:341. These statements seem to seriously challenge the dogmatic equation of glossolalia and unintelligible speech with the oracles of the Greek religion.

[55]Richard Haywood, "The Delphic Oracle," Archaeology, 5 (Summer 1952): 110-18.

[56]Strabo, Geography, 9, iii, 5 in Horace Leonard Jones (trans.), The Geography of Strabo. "The Loeb Classical Library" (8 vols.; William Heinemann, 1927-1932), 4:353.

[57]Plutarch, The Obsolescense of Oracles, 14 in Babbitt, op. cit., 5, 391.

[58]Strabo, Geography, 10, iii, 13, 16 in Jones, op. cit., 5, 99-101, 107.

[59]Strabo, Geography, 10, iii, 15 in Jones, op. cit., 5, 105.

[60]Oesterreich, op. cit., p. 311.

at Delphi.[61] These women who went into an ecstatic state for the purpose of oracular prophecy may well have spoken in *intelligible* language, but nevertheless they were obviously under great emotional strain. Plutarch tells of one Pythia who went berserk, frightening the people who had come to consult the oracle as well as the male interpreters.[62]

The cause of the ecstatic state in Greek religion was artificial and exterior to the person involved. The devotee's wild frenzy may have been induced through the use of wine and drugs. Sometimes use was made of dancing to induce the ecstasy.[63]

Even though the existence of ecstatic, frenzied speech can be documented on the basis of the extant sources, it is too hypothetical to postulate that their speech was *the same as* that in Acts and 1 Corinthians. It appears that the Greeks were ecstatic, but that their speech may have not always been unintelligible. In the contemporary Graeco-Roman world frenzied speech in a religious context was not unusual but rather commonplace. The early Christians may well have known of a religious phenomenon not wholly different from what Luke described in the Pentecost narrative.

GLOSSOLALIA IN THE NEW TESTAMENT

The Greek counterpart of the English term "glossolalia" does not appear in the New Testament; however, the phrase γλώσσαις λαλεῖν does occur.[64] Hence, the English term "glossolalia" is a transliteration of the Greek noun γλῶσσα and

---

[61]Pausanias, *Description of Greece*, 10, xii in W. H. S. Jones (trans.), *Pausanias, Description of Greece*. "The Loeb Classical Library" (5 vols.; Harvard University Press, 1918-1935), 4:431.

[62]Plutarch, *The Obsolescence of Oracles*, 51 in Babbitt, op. cit., 5:499.

[63]Rohde, op. cit., pp. 257-60.

[64]Cf. 1 Corinthians 14:2ff.

the verb λαλεῖν. The term γλῶσσα appears forty-eight times[65] in the canonical New Testament. Although it is commonly translated simply "tongue," it actually has at least three distinct connotations in the New Testament:[66] (1) the physiological organ of taste and/or speech;[67] (2) language;[68] (3) strange or obscure speech.[69]

This latter category claims twenty-five instances of the term, and twenty-four of these are found in Acts and 1 Corinthians.[70] The only other explicit reference to glossolalia contained in the New Testament is Mark 16:17.

And these signs will accompany those who believe; in my

---

[65]Robert Morgenthaler, *Statistik des Neutestamentlichen Wortschatzes* (Gotthelf-Verlag, 1958), p. 85. The number of occurrences is forty-eight if the Nestle text is followed in Acts 2:6. Some witnesses, however, read γλῶσσα instead of διαλέκτω.

[66]Behm, op. cit., 725-26.

[67]Mark 7:33, 7:35; Luke 1:64, 16:24; Acts 2:3, 2:26; 1 Corinthians 14:9; Romans 3:13, 14:11; 1 John 3:18; 1 Peter 3:10; James 1:26, 3:5, 3:6; Revelation 16:10.

[68]Acts 2:11; Revelation 5:9, 7:9, 10:11, 11:9, 13:7, 14:6, 17:5.

[69]Mark 16:17; Acts 2:4, 10:46, 19:6; 1 Corinthians 12:10, 12:28, 12:30, 13:1, 13:8, 14:2, 14:5, 14:6, 14:13, 14:14, 14:18, 14:19, 14:21, 14:22, 14:23, 14:26, 14:27, 14:39. Walter Bauer, *A Greek-English Lexicon of the New Testament and Other Early Christian Literature*, trans. William F. Arndt and F. Wilbur Gingrich (4th rev. ed.; University of Chicago Press, 1952), p. 161. Though the term γλῶσσα does not occur elsewhere, the idea of glossolalia may also be found in 1 Thessalonians 5:19-20; Colossians 3:16; Ephesians 5:18-20. Sometimes it has been suggested that the cry "abba Father" (Rom. 8:15 and Gal. 4:6) is a case of glossolalia as also the phrase "with sighs too deep for words" (Rom. 8:26). Mosiman, op. cit., p. 19, rejects both suggestions as do most other scholars.

[70]Cf. Kenneth Bruce Welliver, "Pentecost and the Early Church" (unpublished doctor's dissertation, Yale University, 1961), pp. 210ff. for a discussion of the references to glossolalia in the fathers.

name they will cast out demons; they will speak in new tongues.

Textual critics are virtually unanimous in the judgment that the authentic text of Mark 16 ends with verse eight.[71] Some neo-Pentecostals willingly accept this textual-critical position. Bastian Van Elderen, for example, concedes:

> In the New Testament the idiom [γλῶσσα λαλεῖν] is found in only two of the twenty-seven books. There is one occurrence in the longer ending of Mark, but on this basis of both internal and external evidence this passage cannot be declared authentic.[72]

The saying preceding the Lord's Prayer in the Sermon on the Mount seems to deprecate any kind of unintelligible utterance in prayer.[73]

> In your prayers do not go babbling on like the heathen, who imagine that the more they say the more likely they are to be heard.[74]

Nevertheless, the gospels records are important in this discussion because they contain references to possession by an "evil" spirit.[75] The cases of ecstatic shouting and madness referred to in the gospels are considered to be *the work of demons*.

---

[71]Cf. Vincent Taylor, *The Gospel According to St. Mark* (Macmillan and Company, 1957), pp. 610, 614-15 and Bruce M. Metzger, *The Text of the New Testament* (Oxford University Press, 1964), pp. 226-29.

[72]Bastian Van Elderen, "Glossolalia in the New Testament," *Bulletin of the Evangelical Theological Society*, 7 (Spring 1964): 53.

[73]Frank W. Beare, "Speaking with Tongues," *Journal of Biblical Literature*, 83 (1964): 229.

[74]Matthew 6:7, *The New English Bible*.

[75]Cf. Mark 1:32, 1:34a, 1:39, 3:11, 3:15, 5:1-20, 6:12-13, 7:25, 9:14-29, 9:38; Matthew 12:22, 12:28, 12:43-45, 10:8; Luke 8:2, 10:20, 11:14-28.

Thus, the ecstaticism that once was regarded as sufficient evidence for the presence and power of God, in the New Testament, is interpreted as an indication of possession by an evil spirit.

Out of such a *Sitz im Leben* arose Acts and 1 Corinthians—the primary sources to be considered in making a theological assessment of the significance of glossolalia in the New Testament. Acts 2 presents the "gift" as a miracle of communication, while in two other instances[76] the writer mentions the phenomenon at crucial junctures in the story of the expansion of the early church. Paul discusses the gift of tongues in a context where he is seeking to set forth the relative value of spiritual gifts.

CONCLUSION

The literature indicates that ecstaticism was not unknown in the history of religious experience. The world view of the Graeco-Roman evidently tolerated these frenzied, ecstatic utterances. Indeed, mankind's longing for God to be on his side and to invest him with divine power has inevitably lead to some type of objective expression whereby the internal power of God may be demonstrated. Certainly, ecstatic speech was one such expression; however, one should not link together earlier instances of ecstaticism to form a lineal descent that leads finally to the New Testament church. But these isolated instances of ecstaticism indicate the presence of frenzied speech *in a religious* context and indicate a religious *milieu* in which ecstaticism was readily acceptable, though not necessarily approved. There is some evidence, however, that by the first century objective phenomena tended to "prove" the indwelling of the spirit were suspect, e.g., these phenomena were considered manifestations of an "evil" spirit.

---

[76]Acts 10:46, 19:6.

3

GLOSSOLALIA IN ACTS

That the *locus classicus* of glossolalia is to be found in Acts 2 is affirmed by the neo-Pentecostals[1] as well as the main stream of Protestantism.[2] In this passage the "gift of tongues" is pictured as being simultaneous with the gift of the Holy Spirit. Luke again mentions the phenomenon at crucial junctures in the story of the expansion of the early church (Acts 10:46, 19:6).

The purpose of this chapter is to set forth a theological exposition of Acts 2:4ff, 10:46, and 19:6. In light of the methodology employed herein such an exposition presupposes not only certain conclusions regarding the results of historical and source criticisms but also a careful assessment of the role of the spirit in the early Christian community.

PROLEGOMENA

In recent years there has been a renaissance of interest in the writings of Saint Luke. Luke-Acts is becoming a focus of

---

[1]William G. MacDonald, *Glossolalia in the New Testament* (Gospel Publishing House, n.d.), p. 1.

[2]Morton T. Kelsey, *Tongue Speaking: An Experiment in Spiritual Experience* (Doubleday and Company, 1964), p. 17.

New Testament studies.[3] Not only are modern scholars rec-
ognizing that Luke's writings comprise twenty-seven per cent
of the New Testament, but also there is a deepening appreciation for the excellence of his work as a theologian. His work
has been characterized as the most interesting and most valuable writing in the New Testament.[4] Since World War II the
focus of Lukan research has shifted from source analysis toward an appreciation of Luke *as theologian*.

Authorship

That Saint Luke, the physician and companion of Paul
(Col. 4:14) was the author of Acts has been the traditional
opinion of the majority of scholars since the late second century. The statement of the anti-Marcionite prologue to Luke is
the basis for this position:

> Luke is a Syrian of Antioch, a doctor by profession. Having
> been a disciple of the Apostles and later having accompanied

---

[3]See Charles H. Talbert, *Luke-Acts: New Perspectives from the Society
of Biblical Literature Seminar* (Crossroads, 1984). Cf. also, C. K. Barrett, *Luke the Historian in Recent Study* (Epworth Press, 1961), p. 50; W.
C. van Unnik, "Luke-Acts, a Storm Center in Contemporary Scholarship," *Studies in Luke-Acts*, Leander E. Keck and J. Louis Martyn,
editors (Abingdon Press, 1966), p. 16. For a survey of recent literature on Acts see Werner Georg Kümmel, "Das Urchristentum,"
Theologische Rundschau, 22 (1954): 191-211. Erich Grässer, "Die Apos-
telgeschiechte in der Forschung der Gegenwart," *Theologische Rundschau*, 26 (1960-1961): 93-167; A. J. Mattill and Mary Benford Mattill
(comp.), *A Classified Bibliography of Literature on the Acts of the Apostles*
(E. J. Brill, 1966); Ward Gasque, *A History of the Criticism of the Acts of
the Apostles* (Eerdmans, 1975); E. Plümacher, "Acta-Forschung 1974-
1982," *Theologische Rundschau*, 48 (1982): 1-56.

[4]Frederick C. Grant, *The Gospels: Their Origin and Their Growth*
(Harper and Row, 1957), p. 133. See, for example, W. S. Kurz, "Luke-
Acts and Historiography in the Greek Bible," *Society for Biblical Literature 1980 Seminar Papers*, Paul Achtemeier, editor (Scholars Press,
1980).

Paul until his [Paul's] martyrdom, he served the Lord without distraction, unmarried, childless, he fell asleep at the age of eighty-four in Boeotia, full of the Holy Spirit.[5]

In addition to the reference in the prologue, Luke is mentioned by name three times in the New Testament. In Philemon 24 he is referred to as a companion of Paul. 2 Timothy 4:11 presents Luke as remaining alone with Paul in prison. Colossians 4:14 characterizes Luke as "the beloved physician."[6]

The question of authorship frequently centers around the "we-sections" of Acts (Acts 16:10-17, 20:5-15, 21:1-18, 27:1-28:16) that have themselves become a "crux of New Testament study."[7] These passages may have been taken from the diary of an individual who was a companion of Paul. There are some

---

[5]Quoted in A. H. McNeile, *An Introduction to the Study of the New Testament* (2nd. ed.; rev. by C. S. C. Williams; Clarendon Press, 1955), p. 29.

[6]The thought of Luke's being a medical doctor has long intrigued scholars. The monumental work in this area is that by William Kirk Hobart, *The Medical Language of St. Luke* (Hodges, Figgis, and Company, 1882). See also Adolf Harnack, *Luke the Physician*, W. D. Morrison, editor; trans. J. R. Wilkinson (G. P. Putnam's Sons, 1907); W. M. Ramsay, "Luke the Physician," *Luke the Physician and Other Studies in the History of Religion* (Hodder and Stoughton, 1908), pp. 1-68; A. T. Robertson, *Luke the Historian in the Light of Research* (Charles Scribner's Sons, 1920). But Henry J. Cadbury, *The Style and Literary Method of Luke*, Parts I and II (Harvard University Press, 1920), p. 50, notes: "The style of Luke bears no more evidence of medical training and interest than does the language of other writers who were not physicians." Feine and Behm, *Introduction to the New Testament*, Werner Georg Kümmel, editor; trans. A. J. Mattill (14th. rev. ed.; Abingdon Press, 1966), pp. 126-30, follow the position of Cadbury.

[7]Henry J. Cadbury, "Acts of the Apostles," *The Interpreter's Dictionary of the Bible*, George Arthur Buttrick, editor (4 vols.; Abingdon Press, 1962), A-D:35. An important recent study is V. Fusco, "Le sezioni-noi degli Atti nella discussione recente," *Bibliotheca Orientalis*, 25 (1983): 73-86.

striking similarities of style and vocabulary to indicate that the "diarist" may also have been the author of the remainder of Luke-Acts.[8]

> There seems no sufficient reason to doubt the unanimous ancient tradition that the author was Luke, the fellow-traveler of Paul, and that the "we" sections are extracts from his personal diary.[9]

Date

The problem of the date of Acts is complicated when it is assumed that Luke-Acts are "companion" volumes written by the same author. This is so because many scholars maintain the priority of Mark over Luke, and, likewise, the fact that Luke precedes Acts. This chronological arrangement—Mark-Luke-Acts—may push the date of Acts into the middle or even late eighties. Yet if Luke wrote Acts this late, the omission of the Neronian persecution of A.D. 64 or the siege of Jerusalem must be explained. Moreover, the author of Acts knows nothing of the later events in the lives of Peter and Paul. Of course, the later the date assigned to Acts the more inexplicable becomes Luke's ignorance of the Pauline corpus.

All of these discrepancies disappear if an earlier date is assigned the book. Many scholars have argued for a date in the early sixties,[10] but how can Acts be a sequel to Luke's gospel if that gospel depends upon Mark?

Assuming the priority of Mark, one possibility is that in Acts 1:1 the "former treatise" refers *not* to the canonical Luke but rather to an earlier edition of that gospel, in all probability

---

[8]Barrett, op. cit., p. 34.

[9]A. Q. Morton and G. H. C. Macgregor, *The Structure of Luke and Acts* (Hodder and Stoughton, 1964), p. 52.

[10]Adolf von Harnack, *The Acts of the Apostles*, trans. J. R. Wilkinson (G. P. Putnam's Sons, 1909), pp. 162-202.

a document not substantially different from proto-Luke identified by B. H. Streeter.[11] This hypothesis would mean that when proto-Luke was written, Luke had not been exposed to the Markan text. On this theory, the rigid chronology of Mark-Luke-Acts is no longer *the* central factor in dating Acts.

Sources

Before 1886 source criticism of Acts consisted almost exclusively of the observation that the "we-sections" were distinct from the remainder of the work.[12] Any theories advanced regarding the sources used were cautiously advanced, and these sources were often thought to be suspect.[13] It was Bernhard Weiss,[14] in 1886, who gave form to the theory of written sources in the first half of Acts; however, little attention was given to the language of Acts. Since the work of Adolf von Harnack,[15] Acts has been viewed as a linguistic unity.[16]

---

[11]In 1921 B. H. Streeter, "Fresh Light on the Synoptic Problem," *The Hibbert Journal*, 20 (1921-1922): 103-12, proposed a theory which was carried forward by Vincent Taylor, *Behind the Third Gospel* (Clarendon Press, 1926). Streeter claimed that Q and L had been combined into "proto-Luke" at some point before the final redaction of the canonical Luke. Cf. B. H. Streeter, *The Four Gospels: A Study of Origins* (Macmillan and Company, 1924), pp. 150-81, 485-562.

[12]Acts 16:10-17, 20:5-15, 21:1-18, 27:1-28:16. For the history of the research on these "we-sections" see Jacques Dupont, *The Sources of Acts*, trans. Kathleen Pond (Darton, Longman and Todd, 1964), pp. 75-93.

[13]F. J. Foakes-Jackson and Kirsopp Lake, *The Beginnings of Christianity: The Acts of the Apostles* (5 vols.; Macmillan and Company, 1922), 2:122-24.

[14]Bernhard D. Weiss, *Einleitung in das Neue Testament* (Wilhelm Hertz, 1886), pp. 569-84.

[15]Harnack, *The Acts of the Apostles*.

[16]Dupont, op. cit., p. 85.

Friedrich Blass[17] and Charles Briggs[18] advanced a single source theory—a Jerusalem source that is to be associated with John Mark. Assuming that the original of Mark ended at 16:8, they posited that Mark himself penned a sequel to his gospel, and that since Luke had used Mark's gospel in preparation of his own, it was only natural to assume that he also used Mark's sequel in the preparation of his sequel.

In 1916 C. C. Torrey advanced the Aramaic theory, which was itself a single source theory.[19] He maintained that Acts 1:2-15:35 is but the translation into Greek of a single Aramaic document. The document was written, avers Torrey, to show how Antioch became the first great gentile center of Christianity. The document was translated by the author of the "we-sections."[20]

---

[17]Friedrich Blass, *Philology of the Gospels* (Macmillan and Company, 1898), pp. 141ff.

[18]Charles Briggs, *New Light on the Life of Jesus* (Charles Scribner's Sons, 1904), pp. 135ff.

[19]C. C. Torrey, *The Composition and Date of Acts* (Harvard University Press, 1916). More recently, cf. Matthew Black, *An Aramaic Approach to the Gospels and Acts* (Clarendon Press, 1946) and R. A. Martin, "Syntactical Evidence of Aramaic Sources in Acts 1-15," *New Testament Studies*, 11 (1964): 38-59.

[20]For criticisms of Torrey's view cf. Edgar J. Goodspeed, "The Origin of Acts," *Journal of Biblical Literature*, 39 (1920): 83-101; F. C. Burkitt, "Professor Torrey on Acts," *Journal of Theological Studies*, 20 (1918): 7; Dupont, op. cit., pp. 27ff. For the view that the author of Luke-Acts subdivides the era of the church into an Apostolic Age and a Post-Apostolic Age, and that there are possibly four such epochs, each passing on authority in the manner of a teacher to his pupil in the philosophic school, see Charles H. Talbert, *Literary Patterns, Theological Themes, and the Genre of Luke-Acts* (Scholars Press, 1970), passim.

While both Friedrich Spitta[21] and Johannes Jüngst[22] advanced dual source theories, it was Harnack who has exercised the greatest influence upon the source criticism of Acts.[23] His theory has been described as "an example of the saner type of source criticism."[24] He made little or no allusion to the work of other investigators, and his ideas were fresh and interesting.

On the basis of the persons and places that comprise each section of Acts 1-15, Harnack posits five separate sources: (1) Jerusalem A source (superior to B)—Acts 3:1-5:16; (2) Jerusalem B source (inferior to A)—Acts 1:6-2:47; (3) Jerusalem-Caesarean source—Acts 8:5-40, 9:31-11:18, 12:1-24; (4) Pauline source—Acts 9:1-30; (5) Antiochene source—Acts 6:1-8:4, 11:19-30, 12:25-15:35.

Harnack believes that the Jerusalem source A is related to the Jerusalem-Caesarean source. This A source, which is derived mainly from men like Philip and Mark, is much superior to the confused and unreliable B source which "combines things that have no real connection with one another, omits

---

[21]Friedrich Spitta, *Die Aspotelgeschichte: Ihre Quellen und deren geschichtlicher Wert* (Vandenhoeck and Ruprecht, 1891). Spitta posited two sources: an A source which contains trustworthy passages (from the pen of Luke) and a B source which contained "supernatural elements" drawn from popular traditions and not nearly so trustworthy as A. These were combined by a redactor, whose influence is apparent.

[22]Johannes Jüngst, *Die Quellen der Apostelgeschichte* (Friedrick Perathes, 1895). Following Spitta, he placed greater emphasis upon the role of the redactor. The B source was held to be an Ebionitic source. It was arranged in Acts so as to agree with A.

[23]Harnack, *The Acts of the Apostles*, pp. 162-202.

[24]G. H. C. Macgregor, "Introduction and Exegesis," *The Interpreter's Bible*, George Arthur Buttrick, editor (12 vols.; Abingdon Press, 1953), 9:18.

what is important, and is devoid of all sense of historical development."[25]

When Harnack speaks of "sources" he is not actually suggesting that these were written sources. On the contrary, after weighing the evidence, he concludes only that they *could* have been written; however, he stresses the *traditions* of individuals, e.g., Philip and Mnason. B. W. Bacon notes that Harnack has helped to unseat the concept of the author of Acts as a "harmonizer." "Luke is not a 'harmonizer.' He is a historical critic of the first magnitude."[26]

Harnack's position has been widely criticized;[27] however, his work has also been most influential.[28] Perhaps the most penetrating criticism of his analysis comes from Bacon, who observed that it is quite impossible to posit the theory of a translator-editor and then presuppose the existence of written documents on the basis of style. "The 'homogeneity' thus established can never go below the surface."[29] W. L. Knox wrote of Harnack's work:

> To sum up the results of our discussion of the sources I would suggest that apart from the speeches . . . which may have been reduced to writing, we have in these chapters no written

---

[25]Harnack, *The Acts of the Apostles*, p. 196.

[26]B. W. Bacon, "Professor Harnack on the Lucan Narrative," *American Journal of Theology*, 13 (1909): 60.

[27]For a critique of Harnack's position see ibid. Cf. Bacon, "More Philological Criticism of Acts," pp. 7-8 and W. L. Knox, *The Acts of the Apostles* (Cambridge University Press, 1948), pp. 19-21.

[28]Cf. Foakes-Jackson and Lake, op. cit., 2:137-57; A. W. F. Blunt, *The Acts of the Apostles* (Clarendon Press, 1922): 24, 25, n. 1, 152, 154; J. A. Findlay, *The Acts of the Apostles: A Commentary* (Student Christian Movement Press, 1934), passim; Roland Schütz, *Apostle und Jünge: Eine quellenkritische und geschichtliche Untersuchung über die Entestehung des Christentums* (Alfred Töplemann, 1921), pp. 15-66.

[29]Bacon, "More Philological Criticism of Acts," p. 17.

sources with the possible exception of chapters 1 to 5 inclusive. . . . [30]

The predominant impression concerning the sources of Acts is certainly negative. He further notes that

despite the most careful and detailed research, it has not been possible to define any of the sources used by the author of Acts in a way which will meet with widespread agreement among the critics.[31]

Conclusions

Any historical work is probably indebted to one or more traditions; however, these may have been either oral or written. Oral traditions can be distinguished from written documents by the existence of contradictions of statements of fact and by the isolation of various methods of presentation. Variation in style does not necessarily constitute the use of oral traditions. If serious differences of language and style can be detected between different parts of a book, written sources, as distinction from oral traditions, may be postulated. But the converse of this argument, i.e., unity of style precludes the use of written sources, is not necessarily true, since the redactor or editor could have rewritten the entire document in his own particular manner.

These observations indicate that the following: (1) most scholars concede that Luke—as any historian—employed sources, although the contents of these sources is widely disputed; (2) many scholars hold that these sources are traceable to the geographical location of their actors;[32] (3) while there is no agreement as to whether these sources were oral or writ-

---

[30]W. L. Knox, op. cit., pp. 100-101.

[31]Dupont, op. cit., p. 166.

[32]Cf. Jüngst, op. cit.; Harnack, op. cit.; Foakes-Jackson and Lake, op. cit.; Martin D. Albertz, *Die Botschaft des Neuen Testamentes* (2 vols.; Evanglischer Verlag, 1952), 1:261-71.

ten, traditionally, source criticism in Acts has centered in Acts 1-15 on the one hand, and the "we-sections" on the other;[33] (4) despite the fact that scholars disagree widely on what verses should be assigned to the various sources, they do agree that the book was not written at one sitting but was probably re-written and edited;[34] (5) Luke's use of sources was always governed by his theological bent.

THE ROLE OF THE SPIRIT IN THE EARLY CHRISTIAN COMMUNITY

The abundance of references to the Spirit in Acts has caused some scholars to concede that the work might well be entitled "The Acts of the Holy Spirit"[35] or "The Activity of the Holy Spirit."[36] No wonder Arnold Ehrhardt claims that the spirit is a "formative principle in the Lukan writings,"[37] and

---

[33]It has been customary to distinguish between the first fifteen chapters which deal with Peter and the Jerusalem church, and the remainder of the book which is given to Paul and his missionary work. Such a breakdown, however, is too rigid, and the distinction between these sections does not hold throughout, e.g., Paul's conversion is found in chapter nine.

[34]Dupont, loc. cit.

[35]Leland Jamison, *Light for the Gentiles* (Westminster Press, 1961), p. 23. Cf. also Miles W. Smith, *On Whom the Spirit Came* (Judson Press, 1948), p. 3.

[36]H. E. Dana, *The Holy Spirit in Acts* (Central Seminary Press, 1943), p. 24. For a similar idea, cf. William Owen Carver, *The Acts of the Apostles* (Sunday School Board, Southern Baptist Convention, 1916), pp. 3, 10.

[37]Arnold Ehrhardt, *The Framework of the New Testament Stories* (Manchester University Press, 1964), p. 89. See G. W. H. Lampe, "The Holy Spirit in the Writings of St. Luke," *Studies in the Gospels*, D. E. Nineham, editor (Blackwell, 1955), pp. 159-200. Cf. also R. Ginns, "The Spirit and the Bride: St. Luke's Witness to the Primitive Church," *Life of the Spirit*, 12 (1957): 16-22, 58-64.

that Josiah Royce observed, Christianity was "from the very start . . . 'a religion of the Spirit.' "[38] A careful study of the Spirit concept in Acts is prerequisite to an understanding of Lukan theology and, specifically, to a theological evaluation of glossolalia.

Antecedents to the Lukan Concept of the Spirit

The Hebraic Background. The most formative influence upon the primitive Christian community lay in its Hebraic background, especially the Old Testament scriptures. The word that is regularly translated "spirit" is רוּחַ though it has other denotative meanings.[39]

The term occurs 378[40] times in the Old Testament, and it has been given a number of translations: "breath," "wind," "spirit," "air," "intellect."[41] The term occurs in the expression, "the Spirit of God," and the Septuagint rendering is πνεῦμα.[42]

From its basic meaning of "wind," רוּחַ was destined to portray the elusive, wind-like,[43] demonic force that was held to ac-

---

[38]Josiah Royce, *William James, and Other Essays on the Philosophy of Life* (Macmillan and Company, 1911), p. 140.

[39]In 131 instances the term means simply "wind." Francis Brown, S. R. Driver and Charles Briggs, *A Hebrew and English Lexicon of the Old Testament* (Houghton Mifflin Company, 1907), pp. 924-25. Cf. H. Wheeler Robinson, *Inspiration and Revelation in the Old Testament* (Clarendon Press, 1946), p. 74; Charles Briggs, "The Use of *'ruach'* in the Old Testament," *Journal of Biblical Literature*, 19 (1900): 132-45.

[40]In addition to the 378 times רוּחַ is used alone, it also appears 94 times in connection with one of the several terms used for God's name.

[41]Brown, Driver and Briggs, op. cit., pp. 924-26.

[42]S. V. McCasland, "Spirit," *The Interpreter's Dictionary of the Bible*, George Arthur Buttrick, editor (4 vols.; Abingdon Press, 1962), R-Z: 433.

[43]Norman H. Snaith, *The Distinctive Ideas of the Old Testament* (Epworth Press, 1953), p. 143.

count for strange and abnormal behavior in humans.[44] Some of
the earliest Old Testament writings use "spirit" as a word to
describe the abnormal.[45] It appears that anything that could
not be brought within the realm of natural causation was attributed to "spirit." Furthermore, this רוּחַ was fundamentally
an activity of God; indeed, it was a gift of God.

The popular interpretation of the idea in its earliest attain-
able form is that of the Spirit of God acting in the extraordinary phenomena of human life.[46]

During the early period the term was an amoral one; therefore, there was nothing incongruous in ascribing the most diverse kinds of behavior to its domination.[47] This fact accounts
for the instance in 1 Samuel 16:14 where a case of homicidal
madness is attributed to "an evil spirit from Yahweh."

A man's vitality depended upon the amount of רוּחַ which
he possessed. This "possession" was thought of in quantita-
tive and not qualitative terms. This non-ethical "energy" has
been referred to as "ruach-Stoff"[48] or "mana."[49] Seen as the

---

[44]J. E. Fison, *The Blessing of the Holy Spirit* (Longmans, Green, and
Company, 1950), p. 61.

[45]Ibid.

[46]I. F. Wood, *The Spirit of God in Biblical Literature* (A. C. Armstrong
and Son, 1904), p. 26. These unaccountable phenomena attributed to
the Spirit may be seen in Judges 6:34 and 14:6.

[47]H. Wheeler Robinson, "Holy Spirit in the Old Testament," *Encyclopedia Britannica* (23 vols.; William Benton, 1962), 11:686.

[48]Paul Volz, *Der Geist Gottes* (J. C. B. Mohr, 1910), p. 23.

[49]Norman H. Snaith, "The Spirit of God in Jewish Thought," *Doctrine of the Holy Spirit*, Vincent Taylor et al, compilers (Epworth Press,
1937), p. 11. Cf. Genesis 1:2; Job 26:13. Edmond Jacob, *Theology of the
Old Testament*, trans. A. W. Heathcott and Philip J. Allcock (Harper
and Brothers, 1958), p. 124, points out how the activity of the Spirit
of God in the early stages of the Old Testament is sporadic, and that
the Spirit acts intermittently and unexpectedly. Cf. Wood, op. cit., p.
26. For further discussion, see Thomas Oliver Kay, "Pentecost: Its
Significance in the Life of the Church" (unpublished master's thesis,
Southern Baptist Theological Seminary, 1954), pp. 31ff.

life-giving, energy-creating power of God, it came and went with no particular regularity. The רוּחַ was the medium through which God exerted his creating and controlling power in the world.[50] That is, God, through the medium of his רוּחַ, not only makes men able for special service but also actually works through men.

As a result of this special endowment of divine power men are able to do that which, relying upon purely human resources, they are incapable of doing.[51]

This "spirit" is the living God himself—the dynamic, creating power of the universe—and not simply a "spirit" *from* him.[52]

The Spirit of God was also thought of as having inspired the prophets, especially the ecstatic ones. One of the more primitive ideas associated with רוּחַ was that an individual could become so possessed by it that he was no longer in control of his faculties. All the great pre-exilic prophets refused to speak of the inspiration of the Spirit.[53] The sparse references in Micah (Micah 2:7, 3:8) and Hosea (Hosea 9:7) sum up the eighth-century contribution.

Sigmund Mowinckel notes that

> the ecstatic element is manifested not in convulsions, delirious frenzy and glossolaly, but in tranquil visions and trances and in the consciousness that they have been given thoughts, words and impulses which do not emanate from themselves.[54]

---

[50]Snaith, *The Distinctive Ideas of the Old Testament*, pp. 154-55.

[51]Fison, op. cit., p. 63.

[52]See Numbers 11:17-29; 1 Samuel 10:6-10, 19:20-23. Since it sometimes inspired the prophet to a frenzied state, it is at times regarded as an evil spirit, as in 1 Samuel 16:15-16, 16:23, 18:10, 19:9; 1 Kings 22:21.

[53]Robinson, *Inspiration and Revelation in the Old Testament*, p. 179.

[54]Sigmund Mowinckel, ' "The Spirit' and the 'Word' in the Pre-Exilic Reforming Prophets," *Journal of Biblical Literature*, 53 (1934): 210.

These classical prophets attributed their message to the "word"; and not to the "Spirit of Yahweh."[55] Consequently, they began to reinterpret the whole meaning of prophecy. רוּחַ was no longer the sole criterion and authentication for the prophet's message; rather, the unique feature was that the "word of God" had come upon him.

Whereas the reforming prophets emphatically stress the fact that they have received Yahweh's word, they do not derive their power from or authenticate their prophetic call by the conception of Yahweh's *ruach*, which, in fact, they have rejected, but by their own consciousness of possessing his word. To them this means a word which is authenticated by expressing Yahweh's own knowledge of God's moral sense.

The major prophets of the seventh and eighth centuries took the spirit-concept out of its association with ecstasy and transformed it from its ethically neutral position into "the concept of the purposeful and deliberate operation of God's personal power."[56] The Spirit of God is seen more clearly as an agent of God, and, furthermore, this God is the God of righteousness, and the Spirit proceeding from Him is a moral energy, operating for moral ends.

There was gradually emerging a distinction between רוּחַ and בָּשָׂר. While it appears that the thought of the prophets was moving toward a personalization of the Spirit of God, this

---

[55]Ezekiel being a true ecstatic of the older type, naturally ascribes his experience to Yahweh's רוּחַ. Cf. Walter Jacobi, *Die Ekstase der alttestamentlichen Propheten* (J. F. Bergmann, 1920), pp. 48ff.

[56]Edward Schweizer, *Spirit of God*, trans. A. E. Harvey (Volume III, Part II of *Bible Key Words* from Gerhard Kittell, editor, *Theologisches Wörterbuch zum Neuen Testament*; Harper and Brothers, 1961), p. 5. John Skinner, *Prophecy and Religion* (Cambridge University Press, 1922), p. 4, warns that "the fact that the great prophets far surpassed their predecessors in their apprehension of religious truth is no reason for denying the reality of the ecstatic element in their experience, or for explaining it away as a mere rhetorical accommodation to traditional modes of expression."

was not achieved in the Old Testament to the degree that it was in parts of the New Testament.

In the tradition of Israel the role of the Spirit was not only connected with the prophet but also with the messianic age to come: ". . . when the Lord shall have washed away the filth . . . by a spirit of judgment and by a spirit of burning" (Is. 4:4). At the coming of that day, God's Spirit will be "poured out," and there will be introduced an age of judgment and blessedness (Is. 32:15-16).

The Messiah himself is to be inspired by the Spirit of God. It is he in whom the elect nation was to find its crown and consummation. It is he who will receive all the gifts of the Divine Spirit in their fullness.

The Messiah is the agent through whom the Spirit of God would be restored upon the messianic people.

The Spirit in Rabbinic Judaism. Although Rabbinic Judaism was prone to relegate the activity of the Spirit to the past, the rabbis still cherished a strong expectation of the coming of the Holy Spirit in the future.[57] In *Numbers Rabba* a rabbi clearly interprets the passage from Joel as an expectation of the age to come: ". . . but in the world to come all Israel will be made prophets, as it is said, (Joel 2:28): . . . 'I will pour out my Spirit upon all flesh.' "[58]

The Spirit in the inter-biblical period. The use of רוּחַ in the apocryphal and pseudepigraphical literature is substantially the same as that of the Septuagint. The term occurs only rarely except in the wisdom literature.[59] In the main, the Spirit is thought to be the spirit of prophecy, primarily in connection with individuals of the past (Sir. 48:12). Contemporary proph-

---

[57]W. D. Davies, *Paul and Rabbinic Judaism* (S.P.C.K., 1948), pp. 205-16.

[58]*Numbers Rabba* 15:25 quoted in Davies, op. cit., p. 216.

[59]William R. Schoemaker, "The Use of 'שׁוּחַ' in the Old Testament and of πνεῦμα in the New Testament," *Journal of Biblical Literature*, 23 (1904): 39-40.

ecy had fallen into disrepute (Zech. 13:2-6), and the Spirit was not "operative" though special inspiration could be granted an individual (2 Esd. 14:22). It was generally acknowledged that prophecy—in the sense of the prophetic spirit—was not to be expected in the present age. 1 Maccabees 4:46 and 14:41 suggested that a "faithful prophet"—i.e., one truly inspired— remained a distant hope. The emphasis was upon the eschatological expectation of a future outpouring of the Spirit on Israel.

The Spirit in the Qumran literature. The literature from Qumran contains several references to the Spirit. The primary use of the term is in connection with the spirits of falsehood and truth that struggle with man.[60] *The Manual of Discipline* contains a developed statement of this concept (3:13-4:26). These spirits appear to be a part of every man, but in the age to come only the spirit of truth will remain (4:18).

Conclusion. The Lukan concept of the Spirit is the Spirit as a sign of the power and presence of God. Progressively the concept took on eschatological dimensions. With every expectation of a fuller and complete revelation, the Old Testament writers turned toward the eschatological future in which Yahweh's self-revelation would issue forth in his Spirit's being "poured out upon all flesh."[61]

The Lukan Concept of the Spirit

As in his gospel, so in Acts, Luke's purpose is to proclaim

---

[60]Millar Burrows, *More Light on the Dead Sea Scrolls* (Viking Press, 1958), pp. 281, 291.

[61]Cf. H. B. Swete, *The Holy Spirit in the New Testament* (Macmillan and Company, 1919), p. 2 and W. S. Bruce, *The Ethics of the Old Testament* (T. & T. Clark, 1895), p. 11. Cf. Albert Curry Winn, "*Pneuma* and *Kerygma*: A New Approach to the New Testament Doctrine of the Holy Spirit" (unpublished doctor's dissertation, Union Theological Seminary, 1956), pp. 356ff.

that salvation is in Jesus Christ.[62] Σωτηρία is the determining factor both in its explicit occurrences and in those instances where implicit reference is made to the idea.[63] In Acts, salvation is seen as both present and future. Thus, in answer to the jailer's question at Philippi, Paul said, "Believe in the Lord Jesus, and you will be saved, you and your household" (Acts 16:31). This emphasis upon the present aspect of salvation does not mean that Luke has substituted *Heilsgeschichte* for eschatology, as if these two ideas were mutually exclusive.[64] On the contrary, he still awaits the one whom God will send to establish "all that God spoke by mouth of his holy prophets from of old" (Acts 3:21b). Luke sees in Jesus the inbreak of eschatological salvation, but the content of that salvation is not exhausted in the present moment.[65]

The concept of μαρτυρία is also central to his writing as evidenced in many of the speeches (Acts 2:32, 3:15, 5:32, 13:31, 20:21, 26:16). The first chapter of Acts projects the idea of "witness," and emphasis is placed upon those "commissioned" to be witnesses. In fact, it has been suggested that Luke presents "doublets" not because of a confusion of sources but rather to make a more reliable case (i.e., a two-fold case) in terms of the

---

[62]Heinrich von Baer, *Der heilige Geist in den Lukasschriften* (Verlag von W. Kohlhammer, 1926), p. 120, observes: "*Der Heilsplan Gottes zur Erlösung der sündigen Nenschheit, das ist Thema des Lukas werkes.*" For a discussion of the theological purpose of Luke-Acts in recent research see H. H. Oliver, "The Lukan Birth Stories and the Purpose of Luke-Acts," *New Testament Studies*, 10 (1963-1964): 203-205.

[63]For a detailed analysis of this theme in Luke see Jacques Dupont, "Le Salut des Gentils et la Signification Théologique du Livre des Actes," *New Testament Studies*, 6 (1959-1960): 132-55.

[64]Cf. Ernst Käsemann, *Essays on New Testament Themes*, trans. W. J. Montagne (Alec R. Allenson, 1964), passim.

[65]Cf. W. G. Kümmel, *Promise and Fulfilment* (SCM Press, 1957), pp. 53ff.

salvation to which he bears witness.[66]

Just as surely as Luke's intention was to proclaim God's salvation and to witness to that reality, so was he convinced that the witness of the Holy Spirit was the ultimate validation of that salvation. Luke mentions the Spirit at every crucial juncture in his dreams of salvation history: at its genesis in Jerusalem, its expansion in Judea, in its invasion of Samaria, in its introduction to the Gentiles at Caesarea and Ephesus, and especially in the life and ministry of Paul who was the symbolic instrument of the outreach of the gospel to the ends of the earth.

In his gospel, Luke stresses how the initial steps of Jesus' ministry are marked by the *power* of the Spirit, e.g., the confrontation of the devil. Subtly, Luke equates δύναμις with πνεῦμα. At several points in the third gospel, Luke intimates that the Spirit will be made available to all Christians at some point in the future. In the meantime, Christians are to pray with expectation that God will bestow his greatest gift, the Holy Spirit. These imitations become clear in the final chapter of Luke's gospel: Jesus assures the disciples that they will be clothed with power from above. This "promise" may be viewed as a connecting link between the gospel and Acts, since the promise is reiterated in the opening verses of Acts. Then in the second chapter of Acts, the promise becomes a reality. It is on the day of Pentecost that the disciples finally realize the fruition of the promise of Jesus.

It was the young Christian community—empowered by the Spirit—that would be the instrument through which would flow the proclamation of the gospel. In ever-widening circles, the gospel would reach "to the ends of the earth." From Jerusalem and Judea through Samaria, no obstacle

---

[66]Paul S. Minear, "Luke's Use of the Birth Stories," *Studies in Luke-Acts*, Leander E. Keck and J. Louis Martyn, editors (Abingdon Press, 1966), p. 114. See also Barrett, op. cit., pp. 37-38 and M. D. Goulder, *Type and History in Acts* (S.P.C.K., 1964), pp. 14-33.

would hinder its progress.[67] Throughout Luke-Acts the intention of the author was to recount the story of salvation that was revealed in Jesus and how that salvation was proclaimed in his ministry and through the Church. His purpose was not merely to record history, however, but to confirm the message of that salvation in his readers. Luke emphasized the role of the Holy Spirit in that context.

By his stress upon the ministry of the Spirit, he testified that the proclamation of the gospel received a divine validation. It was the Spirit that anointed Jesus to proclaim "good news." It was the same Spirit that filled the disciples to speak the word with boldness. It was the Spirit that attested to that proclamation and witness by giving "signs and wonders" at the hands of the Church.[68] Thus, the concept of the Spirit is dominant as a theological motif in Luke-Acts, and it is connected with the purpose of the writings. Specifically, Luke sees the Spirit as one of power.[69] In Luke a theological distinction is to be seen in connection with the Spirit. Not only does he mention the Spirit three times as frequently as Mark, not only does the first half of Acts exhibit the greatest frequency of references to the Spirit to be found in the New Testament, Luke also paves the way for a new understanding of the Spirit.[70]

According to Luke, the coming of the Spirit is known by the observable difference it makes in those who receive it, by manifestations of power, so that they behave in a new way and

---

[67]Cf. the thesis of Frank Stagg, *The Book of Acts* (Broadman Press, 1955), passim.

[68]James R. Bruton, "The Concept of the Holy Spirit as a Theological Motif in Luke-Acts" (unpublished doctor's dissertation, Southern Baptist Seminary, 1967), pp. 235-36.

[69]Cf. Geoffrey Nuttall, "Spirit of Power and Love," *Interpretation*, 4 (1950): 24-35.

[70]Eduard Schweizer, "The Spirit of Power," *Interpretation*, 6 (1952): 264-65.

speak in a new way too. At Pentecost "fear came upon every soul; and many wonders and signs were done through the apostles" (Acts 2:43). "Why do you stare at us," asks Peter at the healing of the lame man, "as though by our own power or piety we had made him to walk?" (Acts 3:12). It was not their own power; but that power was abroad was "manifest to all the inhabitants of Jerusalem, and we cannot deny it," said the authorities (Acts 4:16); and throughout Paul's letters "the power of the Spirit," in which Jesus had entered on his ministry (Luke 4:14), in an echoing phrase. Together with the understanding of the Spirit as one of *power* in action was the strong ethical content which would flow from Paul's letters. In addition the power of the Spirit would issue forth in a new power to speak, just as it did among the Christian forefathers. "Speaking for God," or prophesying, had been a regular effect of the Spirit since the days when the Spirit rested upon Eldad and Medad. So it was in the early church that they were "all filled with the Holy Spirit and spoke the word of God with boldness."

THE RELATIONSHIP OF PENTECOST TO THE EARLY CHRISTIAN COMMUNITY

". . . He charged them not to depart from Jerusalem, but to wait for the promise of the Father . . . " (Acts 1:4). This is the Acts text reflecting the command given by Jesus to his followers. Unfortunately, the text is not specific as to "when" this "promise" is to be fulfilled. Was it simply an accident that the disciples saw this promise fulfilled on the day of Pentecost, or was it within God's providence that this specific day would take on a new meaning? One thing is clear: it is impossible to understand the nature of the primitive Christian community apart from the experience on the day of Pentecost.

The Festival of Pentecost

The day of Pentecost (ἡ πεντηκοστύς) was so called because it was celebrated on the fiftieth day after the presentation of the barley sheaf during the passover observances.[71] It marked the beginning of the offering of the first fruits (Num. 28:26; cf. Ex. 23:16a), and it was known among the Hebrew people as "the feast of weeks" (Ex. 34:22a; Deut. 16:10). Pentecost was one of the three great national festivals during which the male population was required to present itself before the Lord with an offering representative of its means. There is evidence that in the time of Christ multitudes assembled for the Passover, the Feast of Pentecost and the Feast of Tabernacles from Jewish communities scattered throughout the Roman Empire.

The distinctive features of the ritual observed at Pentecost are those of a harvest thanksgiving. The grain harvest lasted seven weeks and was a season of gladness and festivity (Deut. 16:9-11). The harvest season began with the harvesting of the barley during the passover and ended with the harvesting of the wheat, the last cereal to ripen, at Pentecost. Just as the eighth day of tabernacles was the concluding festival of the fruit harvest, so Pentecost was the concluding festival of the grain harvest (Ex. 34:18, 34:22-23).

The Significance of Pentecost in Jewish History

Even though Pentecost evolved out of an agricultural background, it is clear that it later came to be associated with the giving of the law (cf. *Pesahim* 68b). Even though Josephus and Philo do not mention the feast in this connection, the pseudepigraphical work of Jubilees makes the festival as old as Moses. Jubilees 1:1 reads:

And it came to pass in the first year of the exodus of the chil-

---

[71]Pentecost was a colorless name, and, unlike Passover or Unleavened Bread and Tabernacles or Booths, it revealed nothing as to the nature of the festival itself. The term does not occur in the canonical Old Testament; however, it does occur in Tobit 2:1 and 2 Maccabees 12:32. The term appears two other times in the New Testament: Acts 20:16 and 1 Corinthians 16:8. In both cases it functions as a substantive and not an adjective.

dren of Israel out of Egypt, in the third month, on the sixteenth day of the month, that God spake to Moses saying:
'Come up to Me on the mount, and I will give thee two tables
of stone of the law. . . .'

This verse is significant when compared with 6:17:

For this reason it is ordained and written on the heavenly tablets, that they should celebrate the feast of weeks in this
month, once a year, to renew the covenant every year.

It is clear that by the first century the giving of the Law was
commemorated at the feast of Pentecost.

Although the exact day on which the law was given had
long been in dispute, once the giving of the law came to be associated with Pentecost, Talmudic authorities "proved" by the
ingenious calculation that Pentecost was the time at which the
central event occurred. The special lessons of the synagogue
for Pentecost were all designed to glorify the law. "The traditional festival of Pentecost as the birthday of the Torah, when
Israel became a constitutional body . . . remained the sole cel-
ebration of the Exile."[72]

The Significance of Pentecost for the Christian Community

The importance of the Pentecost narrative. The second chapter
of Acts contains a relatively detailed account of the first Christian Pentecost (Acts 2:1-42), i.e., of the first day of Pentecost
after the crucifixion of Jesus. According to the description
given, a series of events took place at that time that added a
uniquely Christian aspect to the ancient Jewish festival. The
position of prominence accorded to this account in relation to
the book as a whole and the striking contrast in the portrayal
of the primitive Christian community before and after the first
pentecost attest to the tremendous value Luke placed upon
the occasion.

---

[72]J. D. Eisenstein, "Pentecost in Rabbinic Literature," *The Jewish
Encyclopedia*, Isidore Singer, editor (12 vols.; Funk and Wagnalls,
1906), 9:593.

The degree of importance of the narrative is indicated, for instance, when Luke relates both preceding and subsequent events to Pentecost. Some of the pre-Pentecost occurrences Luke regards as preparatory to the experience itself. Even in his gospel the event casts its shadow before, and the first chapter of the Book of Acts is clearly intended to lead up to it.[73] For Luke, the Pentecost experience marks not only the point of departure for the Spirit but also the first in a series of "great advances" for the young gospel. "From that moment on the movement was to spread in ever-widening circles."[74] Streeter has observed that

> the New Testament is comparable to an ellipse, which has two foci, rather than to a circle which centers round a single point. This fact is obscured to the ordinary reader by the sheer moral splendor of the Gospel portrait of the Christ. To understand the rise of Christianity we must fix our attention, not only on the personality and teaching of the historic Jesus, but also on the experience spoken of by his followers as the outpouring of the Spirit, which began on the Day of Pentecost next following the Crucifixion.[75]

That the realization of the resurrection was the climax of their experience of the historical Jesus and therefore of the greatest significance to the earliest disciples is hardly debatable. This was the focus around which new hope centered. Here they recovered the Jesus whom they had lost at the Crucifixion. This recovery was, however, short-lived. The post-resurrection ap-

---

[73]Arthur C. McGifferet, *A History of Christianity in the Apostolic Age* (Charles Scribner's Sons, 1897), p. 489.

[74]Morton Scott Enslin, *Christian Beginnings* (Harper and Brothers, 1938), p. 176. That the experience was significant for every member of the group can be readily deduced from the fact that the experience became a "norm" for later converts. Cf. Acts 2:38, 6:3, 8:15-17, 9:17, 10:44-48, 11:15, 19:2-6.

[75]B. H. Streeter, *The God Who Speaks* (Macmillan and Company, 1936), p. 120.

pearances of Jesus were brief; and then, suddenly and unex-
plainably, they ceased. Somehow the contact had been
broken. The new separation, described as the ascension,
meant that the disciples had lost the personal, historical Jesus
again. Following were days of searching and doubt.

The Day of Pentecost, then, marks the second moving
cause of the attitude of the earliest Christians toward Jesus. To
the experience of Easter was added this second great revelation concerning him. Around this second focus centers the
spiritual power manifest in the transformed apostles and in
the apostolic age in general. The genesis of this experience became synonymous with the event of Pentecost itself. These
two events stand side by side in importance for the earliest
Christians.

> To the fact of the Resurrection was added the experience of a
> spirit-filled life; and quite apart from any question as to the
> form in which this experience manifested itself, it is to this
> highly intensified and consecrated perception of God's activ-
> ity in the lives and wills of those who submit themselves to
> Him in Jesus Christ, working on the complex of facts illumi-
> nated by the Resurrection, that the unfolding of systematic
> Christian thinking is due.[76]

The importance of the experience has been recognized by
the Christians of succeeding generations. During the early
centuries of the Christian era, Pentecost was celebrated by the
Greek Orthodox and the Old Catholic churches alike.[77]

Historically and exegetically the place of Pentecost in
Christendom is highly significant.

The purpose of the Pentecost narrative. In light of the discussion of the role of the Spirit in Luke-Acts, as well as the im-

---

[76]C. A. Anderson Scott, "Christ, Christology," *A Dictionary of the
Apostolic Church,* James Hastings, editor (2 vols.; Charles Scribner's
Sons, 1908), 1:183.

[77]B. H. Bruner, *Pentecost: A Renewal of Power* (Doubleday, Doran
and Company, 1928), p. 14.

portance of the Pentecost narrative within that framework, it is obvious that to Luke the Spirit's role on the day of Pentecost is to bestow upon the apostles the *power* needed for the mission which confronts them. From the vantage point of the author, *the Spirit is that power.*

The Pentecost experience has been variously interpreted with regard to its relationship both to the Old Testament and to the future of the Christian community. In terms of its Old Testament significance, Pentecost is sometimes seen as analogous to the giving of the law,[78] reflecting a Jewish tradition that at the giving of the law, God's voice was heard in every language. This tradition took on added significance when the subsequent view emerged that claimed that Pentecost was the feast during which the law was given.[79] Midrash text indicates:

> the ten commandments were announced with a single sound, yet all the people heard the voices, i.e., all the nations of the world heard God in their own language.[80]

Another possibility is that Luke sees in the Pentecost narrative a reversal of the "Tower of Babel" episode. Such a theory has been suggested by R. B. Rackham.[81] Instead of confusion of "tongues" at Pentecost as had been the case at the Tower of Babel there was understanding on the part of

---

[78]For further discussion on the Old Testament and Jewish parallels to Pentecost see Foakes-Jackson and Lake, op. cit., pp. 114ff. and Maurice Barnett, *The Living Flame* (Epworth Press, 1953), pp. 86ff.

[79]F. F. Bruce, op. cit., p. 53.

[80]Elmer H. Zaugg, *A Genetic Study of the Spirit Phenomena in the New Testament* (University of Chicago Press, 1917), p. 51. For the opposite view see "Weeks, Feast of," *The Westminster Dictionary of the Bible*, John D. Davis, editor (Westminster Press, 1944), p. 633 and Swete, op. cit., p. 68.

[81]R. B. Rackham, *The Acts of the Apostles* (Methuen and Company, 1951), p. 53.

each hearer. This theory fits nicely into the context of other considerations concerning Lukan theology and emphasis upon Spirit.

Some conservative scholars regard the Pentecost narrative as the "birthday of the church."[82] While it may be the case that Luke sought to draw a parallel between the birth of the Messiah in his gospel and of the church in Acts (each being the result of the work of the Spirit) a theological analysis of "church" is required for a significant probing of the issue.[83] Certainly, the gathered community existed from the time that Jesus was confessed as the Messiah. In fact, the outpouring of God's Spirit at Pentecost is related to the church, like the presence of the Spirit to Jesus at his baptism: the Son of God is only fully commissioned as Messiah at the time of the anointing, just as the church is only fully commissioned as the messianic community at Pentecost. Thus the disciples did not become the church at Pentecost any more than Jesus became the Son of God at his baptism.

Another option is to assess the narrative in terms of the *empowering* of the church that in fact already existed. God's election now embraces the Christian community—the new Israel, the people of God.[84] God empowered those Christians

---

[82]Philip Schaff, *History of the Christian Church* (8 vols.; Charles Scribner's Sons, 1882-1910), 1:225. Vernon Bartlet, *The Acts* (Oxford University Press, 1902), p. 135; G. Campbell Morgan, *The Acts of the Apostles* (Revell, 1924), p. 24.

[83]For a detailed statement of the validity of the ἐκκλησία statements in Matthew 16:18 and 18:17 see Karl Ludwig Smith, *The Church*, trans. J. R. Coates (Volume I, Part 11 of *Bible Key Words* from Gerhard Kittel (ed.), *Theologisches Wörterbuch zum Neuen Testament*; Harper and Brothers, 1961), pp. 35ff. Cf. Oscar Cullmann, *Peter* (Westminster Press, 1953), pp. 184-212 and R. Newton Flew, *Jesus and His Church* (Epworth Press, 1938), pp. 35-88. On the various theories as to the time of the origin of the church see J. Robert Nelson, *The Realm of Redemption* (Wilcox and Follett Company, 1951), pp. 1-36.

[84]H. H. Rowley, *The Biblical Doctrine of Election* (Lutterworth Press, 1950), pp. 139-74.

through the *power* of his Spirit. The coming of the Spirit is attended by the sound "like the rush of a mighty wind" and "tongues as of fire." Both of these analogies were associated with the Spirit in Rabbinic Judaism.[85] Both of these phenomena denote the ancient understanding of the Spirit's operation as *power*,[86] and the physical manifestation which these two elements constitute was a definite sign to the church that the Spirit had come, and consequently, these are to be considered as constituent parts of the miracle.[87] Despite the difficulties for the modern mind, this amazing inbreak of supernatural power at Pentecost caused little or no surprise among the participants. Luke indicates in Acts 1:4-5 that they "knew that this was the fulfillment of the Lord's promise of fuller life and power, a promise made repeatedly during his ministry and just before he disappeared from sight."[88] The citation of Joel's prophecy indicates that the event was regarded as a renewal of the Old Testament gift of prophecy; however, in this case, not to a select few, but rather to all believers alike.

The gift of the Holy Spirit as the normal endowment of every baptised believer, in contrast with the abnormal intermittent

---

[85]Cf. Davies, op. cit., p. 184 and J. Abelson, *The Immanence of God in Rabbinic Literature* (Macmillan and Company, 1912), pp. 212ff.

[86]Abraham Kuyper, *The Work of the Holy Spirit*, trans. Henri De Vries (Funk and Wagnalls Company, 1900), p. 32, contends that the wind and tongues of fire are of the same essential relationship with the Spirit as the speaking in tongues, but that the former were demonstrated only at Pentecost since it was the only instance of the coming of the Spirit in the life of the church. In the case of the experience at the home of Cornelius, Kuyper notes that this was not a "coming" but rather a "conducting" of the Spirit into another part of the Body of Christ; therefore, the tongues of fire and the wind are not repeated but only the speaking in tongues.

[87]Ibid., pp. 128ff.

[88]Allan J. MacDonald, *The Interpreter Spirit and Human Life* (S.P.C.K., 1944), p. 131.

endowment of individuals for special activity or work, was reserved for the time when the incarnation should be completed, and mankind and the new Christian church, especially, should be placed finally under the Spirit's guidance and influence.[89]

Thus, the primitive church was a community of people who believed themselves to have been given the power of God *through* his Spirit which was poured out upon them after the exaltation of Christ. The various abnormal phenomena attested to the Spirit's invasion of their lives. From observable effects these early Christians deduced causes. The inevitable conclusion was that the same power which operated in and through the person of Jesus Christ was now "poured out" upon them. Features that may be regarded today as "unusual" cannot be dismissed as hysteria or pathological disturbances. To the mind steeped in traditional Jewish psychology they were themselves demonstrations of a stirring awakening.[90]

THE PRIMARY REFERENCES TO TONGUES IN ACTS

Tongues at Pentecost

Traditional interpretations. The details of the glossolalia occurrence embedded in the Pentecost narrative are not so clear as one might wish. That there are more questions than answers is abundantly clear.[91] Of the many problems[92] connected

---

[89]Ibid., p. 32.

[90]Barnett, op. cit., p. 59.

[91]Stagg, op. cit., p. 54.

[92]The question is immediately raised as to who was "filled with the Holy Spirit." Lindsay Dewar, *The Holy Spirit and Modern Thought* (A. R. Mowbray and Company, 1959), p. 58, limits the "all" to the apostles. W. H. Griffith Thomas, *The Holy Spirit and Modern Thought* (Eerdmans, 1955), p. 40, maintains that the narrative does not warrant the limitation suggested by Dewar. F. F. Bruce, op. cit., p. 88, holds that all the believers received the gift of the Spirit, but only the twelve presented themselves to the populace as the leaders.

with the account, none is more baffling than that concerning the reference to "other tongues" in Acts 2:4. Does the expression ἑτέραις γλώσσαις here refer to "other languages" as the eighth verse seems to indicate? There are at least three possibilities:

(1) The tongues represent intelligible speech. Those who adhere to this interpretation point out that there is little doubt that on the day of Pentecost, something powerful united a group of dispairing individuals and sent them into a pagan world as crusading champions. Embedded in this drama is the reference to a glossolalia that was understandable and to a crowd of people who came from many different language groups.[93] Thus, historically many interpreters have understood the tongues to refer to foreign languages.

The early church fathers, for example, commonly advanced the interpretation that the tongues were foreign languages.[94] Irenaeus notes that there are "many brethren in the Church, . . . who through the Spirit speak all kinds of languages. . . ."[95] His statement likely refers to tongues understood as foreign languages. Augustine observes:

---

[93]Barnett, op. cit., p. 82. Glossolalia as a foreign language was rejected as early as 1898. Cf. Carl Clemen, "The 'Speaking with Tongues' of the Early Church," *Expository Times*, 10 (1898): 344-52.

[94]It was not until the 1928 American Prayer Book that the phrase "the gifts of divers languages" was omitted. Cf. Massey H. Shepherd (ed.), *The Oxford American Prayer Book Commentary* (Oxford University Press, 1950), pp. 77-78.

[95]Irenaeus, *Against Heresies*, V, vi, 1 in Philip Schaff (ed.), *Ante-Nicene Fathers* (10 vols.; Charles Scribner's Sons, 1908), 1:531. Consistent, but not identical, with this tradition, the fathers generally believed that the disciples at Pentecost were miraculously and permanently endowed with the power to use foreign languages in their missionary endeavors. Origen, Gregory of Niziansus, Gregory of Nyssa, Jerome, and others held that interpretation of Pentecost. Cf. Joseph R. Estes, "The Biblical Concept of Spiritual Gifts" (unpublished doctor's dissertation, Southern Baptist Seminary, 1957), pp. 44-45.

> Every one of them spoke in tongues of all nations; thus sig-
> nifying that the unity of the Catholic Church would embrace
> all nations, and would in like manner speak in all times.[96]

Eusebius of Emesa writes:

> But when he gave literary ability to ignorant men so that they
> could write gospels, giving the ability to write he also gave
> the Roman tongue to Galileans, and the languages of the
> world to his apostles, for the teaching and admonition and ex-
> hortation of the nations of the world.[97]

Besides ancient support this theory enjoyed some popu-
larity in more recent years.[98] Miles Smith goes so far as to con-
clude that the Pentecost narrative will admit to no other
interpretation.[99] Other interpreters suggest that even though
Luke might have misunderstood the "actual" event, he clearly
understood the tongues as utterances in foreign languages.[100]

---

[96]Augustine, *The City of God*, 18, 49 in Philip Schaff (ed.); *Nicene
and Post-Nicene Fathers* (first series, 14 vols.; Eerdmans, 1956), 2:191.
Cf. Chrysostom, *Homily*, 35 in Schaff (ed.), *Nicene and Post-Nicene Fathers*, 12:201.

[97]Eusebius of Emesa quotes in Kenneth Bruce Welliver, "Pentecost and the Early Church" (unpublished doctor's dissertation, Yale
University, 1961), p. 210.

[98]Cf., for example, Horatio B. Hackett, *Commentary on the Original
Text of the Acts of the Apostles* (Gould and Lincoln, 1858), pp. 51ff. and
Herman Olshausen, *Biblical Commentary on the Gospels and on the Acts
of the Apostles* (4 vols.; T. & T. Clark, 1847-1850), 4:372ff.

[99]Miles W. Smith, op. cit., p. 22.

[100]Barnett, op. cit., p. 82; Foakes-Jackson and Lake, op. cit., p.
112; William G. Moorehead, "Tongues of Fire," *The International Standard Bible Encyclopedia* (5 vols.; Howard-Severance Company, 1915),
5:2997; J. Rawson Lumby, *The Acts of the Apostles* (Cambridge University Press, 1912), p. 95.

Arthur Wright attempts to defend tongues as foreign languages by citing a more recent example. He points out that the "little prophets of the Cevennes" (1687-1701) preached at length in acceptable French instead of their native dialect.[101] Though not ecstatic their discourses could not be stopped. Wright explained the phenomenon by claiming that the children were repeating sermons they had heard previously; therefore, for Wright, the Pentecost narrative merely attributes to the primitive Christians the ability to repeat what they had heard at earlier feasts. They contributed no distinctively Christian teachings but rather recited the "mighty works of God" in many unknown languages.[102]

Probably the most serious advocate of this position in the twentieth century is Dawson Walker.[103] He develops his case as follows: (1) The term γλῶσσα may mean by itself, either a foreign word or foreign speech in the use of the Attic writers. (2) Since Paul refers to "kinds of tongues" a variety of tongue

---

[101]Arthur Wright, *Some New Testament Problems* (Muthuen and Company, 1898), p. 269. Wright further contends that there is no necessary contradiction between the account in Acts and Paul's discussion in 1 Corinthians. Cf. ibid., p. 285. For the opposite view see Burton Scott Easton, "Tongues, Gift of," *The International Standard Bible Encyclopedia* (5 vols.; Howard-Severance Company, 1915), 5:2994 and Lumby, loc. cit. Ingenious efforts have been made to explain the alleged gift of foreign languages in psychological terms. Lindsay Dewar, "The Problem of Pentecost," *Theology*, 9 (1924): 253, claims that the tongues were fragments of Hebrew texts, learned and suppressed into the subconscious of the apostles until they were released at the Spirit's coming.

[102]Émile Lombard, *De la Glossolalie chez les premiers Chrétiens* (Bridel, 1910), p. 71, concludes that all purported cases of xenoglossolalia are of individual persons preaching to a group, not a collective assembly all manifesting the gift simultaneously. It is not beneficial to the interpreter, therefore, to establish this concept in Acts.

[103]Dawson Walker, *The Gift of Tongues and Other Essays* (T. & T. Clark, 1906), pp. 40-42.

speech is indicated. (3) Paul's use of Isaiah 28:11 assumes that foreign language is an admissible interpretation of tongues. (4) The "interpreter" could be simply a person who is conversant in the given language.

There are several problems inherent in Walker's interpretation. First, he cites little linguistic support for his interpretation of the meaning of the term γλῶσσα. Many scholars would not favor such a translation.[104] The fact that Paul speaks of "kinds of tongues" could simply mean that there were many different dialects; however, it might also indicate that there were many varieties of tongues, some genuine, some not, and that Paul refused to condemn them in toto. Such an interpretation would account for Paul's apparent ambivalence regarding glossolalia. The most serious flaw in Walker's argument, however, is the fact that his case presupposes that the glossolalia at Pentecost and Corinth is the same phenomenon. Walker is using Paul's comments to support his contention that the Pentecost narrative should be understood as referring to foreign languages. Again, it should be noted that his argument is in reality primarily a defense of the historicity of the Pentecost narrative, and only secondarily germane to his considerations of glossolalia. He concludes:

> The demonstration of this view, that foreign languages were spoken in ecstasy at Corinth as well as at Jerusalem, is not essential for the establishing of the view which we are here seeking to support. . . . But if . . . this variety of the gift was displayed at Corinth also, it immensely strengthens the

---

[104]Cf. Joseph Henry Thayer, *A Greek-English Lexicon of the New Testament* (4th ed.; T. & T. Clark, 1901), p. 116; G. Abbott-Smith, *A Manual Greek Lexicon of the New Testament* (3rd. ed.; T. & T. Clark, 1937), p. 93. Bauer-Arndt-Gingrich, op. cit., Walter Baür, *A Greek-English Lexicon of the New Testament and Other Early Christian Literature*, trans. William F. Arndt and F. Wilbur Gingrich (4th. rev. ed.; University of Chicago Press, 1952), p. 161; Johannes Behm, "γλῶσσα," *Theological Dictionary of the New Testament*, Gerhard Kittel, editor; trans. Geoffrey W. Bromily (10 vols.; Eerdmans, 1964-1976), 1:719ff.

case in favour of St. Luke, and provides additional grounds for regarding his narrative as reliable.[105]

Finally, in his sermon Peter links the occurrences of Pentecost with the rebirth of the gift of prophecy; however, in the Old Testament prophecy is never associated with foreign languages. H. A. W. Meyer concludes that "the sudden communication of a facility of speaking foreign languages is neither logically possible nor psychologically and morally conceivable."[106]

Another theory is that the glossolalia at Pentecost was not extended discourse but rather "intermittent" foreign language. According to this theory a case of heightened memory as a result of the emotional experience at Pentecost, and, as a result, they were able to speak intermittently in foreign phrases which they had heard earlier.

> The phrases and sentences in the foreign languages were in all probability only the flotsam and jetsam of the general current of speech. They came to the surface occasionally, and they doubtless repeated again and again. The most of the speaking was unintelligible, . . . but these foreign phrases spoken by Galileans who were not linguists and clearly understood by the foreigners of many nations, were the remarkable feature of the phenomenon at Pentecost; and this is the remarkable feature which Luke has taken care to record.[107]

---

[105]Walker, op. cit., p. 42.

[106]H. A. W. Meyer, *Kritisch Exegetisches Handbuch über die Apostelgeschichte* (Vandenhoeck und Ruprecht, 1870), p. 48.

[107]Doremus Almy Hayes, *The Gift of Tongues* (Jennings and Graham, 1913), pp. 60-61. Kirsopp Lake, *The Earlier Epistles of Paul* (Rivingtons, 1911), pp. 242-47, cites parallel examples from the Testament of Job, where the daughters of Job are reported to have spoken in different types of tongue languages: one speaks in the angelic tongue; the second in the tongues of principalities; the third in the tongue of "those on high."

A variation is offered by Kirsopp Lake who suggests that the glossolalia at Pentecost, while possibly interspersed with foreign words and phrases, was different from "foreign languages" in the usual sense. He concludes that the tradition of the "foreign languages" is but

> an attempt by a friendly editor, separated from the actual event, to explain the glossolalia, just as the charge of drunkenness was the attempt of unfriendly observers, separated by a lack of sympathy.[108]

Lake thinks that the Pentecost narrative as it is in canonical Acts may well be a redaction of an early document, made by a member of the Pauline school, who did not fully understand it, but who was imbued with the Pauline distrust of unintelligible glossolalia.[109]

(2) The miracle is in the hearing. Another group of scholars maintains the Pentecost narrative represents not a miracle of speech, but one of hearing.[110] Viewing the entire episode as supernatural, these scholars believe that the specific miracle is not the glossolalia but rather the understanding which resulted from it. George Cutten[111] contends that the speech itself was unintelligible to the ordinary hearer, but the gift of the Spirit brought about understanding. Obviously, emphasis is placed upon the fact that in verse 8 the narrative clearly sug-

---

[108]Foakes-Jackson and Lake, op. cit., p. 120.

[109]Ibid., p. 118.

[110]Gregory of Nazianzen was the first to consider the possibility of this interpretation, though he ultimately rejected it himself in favor of the traditional view. Cf. Gregory of Nazianzen, *Oration XLI*, "On Pentecost" in Philip Schaff (ed.), *Nicene and Post-Nicene Fathers* (second series, 14 vols.; Eerdmans, 1952), 7:378-85.

[111]George B. Cutten, *Speaking with Tongues: Historically and Psychologically Considered* (Yale University Press, 1927), passim. Cf. Schaff, *History of the Christian Church*, 1: 230-32.

gests that the spectators *heard* in their own native languages; it is not asserted that the *speaking* was in their native language.

E. F. Scott holds a similar position. Noting that the other references to tongue speech in Acts give no suggestion of foreign languages Scott suggests that Luke, while fully aware that the "tongues" were unintelligible, believed, in common with many of his contemporaries, that they were real languages.[112] The curious term, γλώσσαις λαλεῖν, applied to the phenomenon indicates that they were considered true languages in some sense. The meaning of the term can hardly be other than that implied in Luke's narrative—that the speaker employed languages, though not necessarily foreign languages, Scott concludes.[113]

This interpretation hinges upon the verb ἀκούειν. Some grammarians propose that this verb sometimes retains the classical distinction of cases: the genitive meaning "to understand" and the accusative meaning "to hear."[114] Thus the meaning of ἀκούειν in Acts 2:6b, 8 and 11 is actually "to understand" since in both 6b and 11, where the noun object occurs, it is in the genitive case. This interpretation points out that there seems to be two groups who gather in the crowd: the "devout men" (εὐλαβής) and the "others" (ἕτεροι) who mock. It is the former group of pious men who understand the glossolalia as their "own native language," not the critical mockers. Thus the miracle becomes not one of speaking but of hearing. Although this theory of the Pentecostal experience is highly attractive, certain problems arise which should be noted.

First, on the basis of the narrative itself, it appears superficial to divide the crowd into two groups. It is natural to as-

---

[112]E. F. Scott, op. cit., pp. 96ff.

[113]*Ibid.*, p. 99.

[114]A. T. Robertson, *A Grammar of the Greek New Testament in the Light of Historical Research* (2nd. ed.; George H. Doran Company, 1915), pp. 506-507.

sume that all diaspora Jews who would gather in Jerusalem for the feast might be called "devout" men. Luke gives the impression that the entire crowd heard in their own languages. The term ἕκαστος occurs in verses 6 and 8, while πάντες appears in verse 12.

The narrative itself does not betray the fact that Luke thought any miracle was connected with the hearing of the glossolalia. He does not indicate that the gift of the Spirit descended upon the crowd.[115] He makes no mention of any interpreting or translating taking place. It is highly unlikely that any "detached" observer who was not himself caught up in the apostolic band would presume to interpret what was being said.

Finally, it appears that Luke's emphasis was in fact upon the speaking and not the hearing. He indicates in verses 6 and 8 that this speech (φωνῆς) was being uttered even before the crowd had assembled. According to the extant narrative, possibly it was *because* the Jews recognized their native dialects that they gathered.

(3) The tongues are totally unintelligible. A final group of scholars asserts that the Pentecost narrative is virtually invalid, and that the glossolalia, if indeed there were such a phenomenon, was totally unintelligible. The logical end of this position is the affirmation that the original text has become corrupted, or simply that the event itself is a fabrication.

Maurice Goguel is representative. He contends that the Jerusalem church was non-pneumatic in its nature while pneu-

---

[115]Another ingenious suggestion has been made by George A. Barton, *Archaeology and the Bible* (7th ed.; American Sunday School Union, 1937), p. 12, who considers the phenomenon a matter of hearing but without any miraculous element. He suggests that the sounds omitted by the glossolalists were understood by the hearers of words and phrases of their native languages. Many syllabic sounds have different meanings in various languages. He illustrates the point with the sound "bad" which can have different interpretations in English, German, Hebrew, Arabic and French.

matism was peculiar to Greek Christianity.[116] Goguel asserts that the canonical record of glossolalia in Acts is the result of the author's attempt to describe the outburst of glossolalia; however, since the event was not current in his own time, he was forced to form his own idea of what glossolalia signified. In doing so, avers Goguel, he not only misunderstood the phenomena, but he imposed it upon the Jerusalem church which was in reality opposed to such phenomena.

There can be only one essential phenomenon known as glossolalia. A real problem emerges when it is assumed that Luke equates glossolalia with foreign languages and Paul obviously does not. One way of dealing with the resultant contradiction is to regard Luke's record as the conflation of two or more sources. Harnack regards Acts 3:1-5:16 as the primitive narrative, while relegating Acts 2 and 5:17-42 to the role of a legendary recension of the same events.[117] This "doublet theory" has attracted much attention; and though it certainly represents an ingenious bit of scholarship, it has yet to receive wide acceptance among New Testament scholars.

A large number of scholars follow a source theory that Lake has succinctly summarized.[118] This theory eliminates Acts 2:5-11 from the text, regarding it as a later elaboration of a simple case of ecstatic and meaningless glossolalia. This notion arises because verses 7 and 12 appear to be doublets, and because Peter apparently makes no reference to a miracle of speaking in foreign languages.

Some researchers feel that the source theory explanations raise more problems than they solve.[119] The problem could be

---

[116]Maurice Goguel, *The Birth of Christianity*, trans. M. C. Snape (Macmillan and Company, 1954), pp. 95ff.

[117]Harnack, *The Acts of the Apostles*, pp. 179-83, 188-89.

[118]Foakes-Jackson and Lake, op. cit., 5:118-20. See also Barnett, op. cit., p. 84. Cf. Macgregor, op. cit., pp. 39ff.

[119]Arthur Adams Lovekin, "Glossolalia: A Critical Study of Alleged Origins, the New Testament and the Early Church" (unpublished master's thesis, University of the South, 1962), pp. 74ff.

rectified quite apart from elaborate source analysis. The troublesome part of the narrative is not a "part" at all—it is simply the term διάλεκτος, i.e., Luke asserts that each heard in his own "language." The discussion of "doublets" is intriguing, to be sure; but much more central is Luke's echo of the charge that the disciples were inebriated, if indeed he claims for them foreign speech.

The specific areas where the interpretation of tongues in Acts becomes problematic may be summarized as follows:

(1) Nowhere else in the New Testament is the glossolalia understood as the ability to speak in foreign languages. Although Paul, for the sake of illustration, compares the tongues at Corinth with foreign languages,[120] his basic contention is that no one is able to understand them. Furthermore, the author of Acts records other instances of glossolalia,[121] and in none of these is it stated or implied that foreign languages were involved. On the contrary, it is implied that these later occurrences were identical in nature with what happened at Pentecost: "God gave the same gift to them as he gave to us";[122] "God . . . bore witness to them, giving them the Holy Spirit just as he did to us."[123]

(2) The miracle of foreign languages is not even consistently maintained in the Pentecost narrative itself. Some of those present said, "They are filled with new wine."[124] This is not the impression that foreign languages would have made. Further, when Peter begins to preach, he takes his start from the accusation of drunkenness, and he never mentions foreign languages. His introduction presupposes that everyone has

----

[120]1 Corinthians 14:10-11.

[121]Acts 10:46, 19:6.

[122]Acts 11:17.

[123]Acts 15:8.

[124]Acts 2:13b. A similar impression of glossolalia appears to have been made at Corinth. Cf. 1 Corinthians 14:23.

not understood what was said. This consideration has suggested the possibility that verses 5 through 11 represent a redaction of the original narrative.

(3) There are other indications that suggest that the canonical record of the Pentecost event has been edited and/or conflated. The catalog of nations does not include "every nation under heaven"—the Greek homelands, Macedonia and Achaia are conspicuously missing. Nor is it likely that Jews living in those various places would know the ancient local dialects, since either Aramaic or Greek was the common language of the people in all those places named. Certainly the Jews would term such local dialects as did survive "our own tongues." Moreover, the gift of foreign languages would have been useless since Peter preaches a sermon in Aramaic, and everyone understands him.

In the face of these difficulties, there are at least three possible solutions:

(1) Heinrich Weinel[125] maintains that Acts was written so late that the author was no longer familiar with the actual details of the event. Unable to understand his source, he invented the explanation of foreign languages.

(2) E. F. Scott[126] acknowledges that Luke was quite familiar with glossolalia as it occurred in the early church. But in this instance, Luke was carried away with his love for symbolism. Scott cites the rejection at Nazareth[127] as an expression of a historical event, dressed out by Luke's imagination to serve as a frontispiece for the gospel, signalizing the ultimate rejection of Jesus by his own people. Similarly, the Pentecost narrative has been dressed out as the frontispiece of Acts, to signal the ultimate reception of the gospel by men of all nations.

---

[125]Heinrich Weinel, *Die Wirkungen des Geistes und der Geister im nachapostolischen Zeitalter bis auf Irenaüs* (J. C. B. Mohr, 1899), pp. 74ff.

[126]E. F. Scott, op. cit., p. 96.

[127]Luke 4:16-30.

(3) The other possible solution is that there has been an interpolation in the midst of an originally self-consistent narrative. Luke may or may not have made this interpolation. For the moment, let the reader assume that Luke or a later editor in fact did insert the foreign language motif into the Pentecost narrative. With this assumption, it would be possible to assess the Pentecost narrative for *meaning*, without becoming bogged down regarding the external, formal structure of the glossolalia.

A Reconstruction

The "theological" intent of Acts, in the final analysis, is to demonstrate that the gospel is dependent, neither upon Peter nor Paul, nor the twelve, but rather upon a superhuman power—the Spirit of God. In light of its background in the Old Testament and its role of the early church, the Spirit was not something that welled up within man, as a part of his natural endowment. Rather, it was that ineffable, external force that transcended his being and touched him to the very depths of his being.

> The phenomena accompanying its manifestations were of the kind that we associated with early prophetism, with its corybantic ravings, that moved those who beheld them to amazement sometimes not unmixed with disgust.[128]

Even if the question as to whether the tongues were a foreign language or not could be resolved, there would remain unanswered the larger—and central—question of *meaning*. It is clear in light of the previous discussion that glossolalia should not be understood *simply* as foreign languages, though they may be this: the main consideration is that one does not lose sight of that force which turned this unique phenomena into a meaningful event. In Luke's eyes this "force" was none other than the Spirit of God. It was this Spirit who empowered

---

[128]C. R. North, *The Thought of the Old Testament* (Epworth Press, 1948), p. 40.

the apostles for the missionary work of gospel; He supported them in their preaching; He was the chief witness of the truth of the gospel.

It is not the case that the author of Acts had a "naive interest in the miraculous" or in the abnormal psychic phenomena attending the Spirit's working, but rather, since these manifestations are the natural accompaniment of the Spirit, he simply sought to report the workings of the Spirit in their context. Of the abnormal manifestations which are enumerated in Acts, the special speech phenomena took first place.[129] While it is true that the glossolalia was neither properly didactic nor properly practical, there was, no doubt, some kind of communication within the context of the community. Wayne Oates notes that actual, intelligible language is not always necessary for communication and understanding.

> Each man was able to capture the meaning of the other. There was a subsoil of devoutness in the audience, for the text says that those who were present were "devout men from every nation under heaven." Earl Loomis, . . . has called the process of non-verbal, subverbal, and superverbal understanding *resonance*. Of course, its opposite is *dissonance*. One can by analogy see this in the reaction of music instruments to each other. For example, two tuning forks of the same kind will both vibrate when one is struck. Among human beings the *consciousness of kind*, or the feeling of kinship, produces a sympathetic vibration between people. The gift of the Holy Spirit energizes this kind of understanding between people. This understanding is highly idiosyncratic—each understands it his own way. It is highly communal—those who understand each other eat together in gladness and singleness of heart. This understanding is reciprocal—no one person is left to do all the understanding in one-way communication.[130]

---

[129]Barnett, op. cit., p. 58.

[130]Wayne E. Oates, "The Holy Spirit and the Overseer of the Flock," *Review and Expositor*, 63 (Spring 1966): 168. Cf. Reuel Howe, *The Miracle of Dialogue* (Seabury Press, 1963), p. 106.

Certainly psychological motivations that might have triggered such a response at Pentecost were abundant: the realization that Jesus had been resurrected; increasing fear of the Jewish authorities; and the inward realization that God's Spirit was present. This kind of "transcendent" communication would reconcile the difficult problem posed by Luke's use of δι-αλέκτῳ in verses 6 and 8.

Luke, then, means to say that to the group of Jesus' disciples who were gathered at the Pentecostal festival there came a soul-shaking experience which they—and he—interpreted as the outpouring of the Spirit of God upon them. The external form, however explained, is but a witness to the extraordinary character of the event itself. Moreover, the subsequent behavior of the disciples is sufficient testimony to its lasting effect upon them.

> They were convinced that their Master Jesus had been raised from the dead and exalted to the throne of the Messiah by the power of God. Being thus exalted, he had poured out his Spirit upon the members of his own community. They could now go forth in the power of that same Spirit to continue his Messianic work in the world.[131]

This appears to be the central claim of Acts, and this contention is supported in other New Testament books. 1 Peter reflects a similar motif:

> But rejoice insofar as you share Christ's sufferings, that you may also rejoice and be glad when his glory is revealed. If you are reproached for the name of Christ, you are blessed, because the spirit of glory and of God rests upon you (1 Pet. 4:13-14).

This passage clearly links the messianic community with the Messiah himself. Just as the community shares his sufferings, likewise it shares his Spirit.

---

[131]F. W. Dillistone, "The Biblical Doctrine of the Holy Spirit," *Theology Today*, 3 (1946-1947): 493.

> You are the messianic community and you therefore par-
> take of the Spirit which rests upon the Messiah. You are one
> with Christ in all things messianic. You share the Name, the
> Glory, and the Spirit.[132]

A similar thought is found in Hebrews where those who had
become partakers of the Messiah are reminded that they are
also partakers of the Holy Spirit.[133] Moreover, in the writings
of Paul, the thought comes to even fuller expression. It is a
fundamental principle for Paul that through the agency of the
Holy Spirit the graces and gifts of the Messiah are reproduced
in his people. The Spirit manifested in the Messiah was being
further manifested in the members of his body.

The general framework of the biblical record is clear. The
Spirit is preeminently the title applied to God in action. Before
Christ, the Spirit came upon chosen men, inspiring and con-
straining them to share in divine activity in word and deed.
Gradually, a hope emerged of a new age when God's chosen
servant—the Messiah—the Spirit would rest in an altogether
unparalleled manner, and when participation in the Spirit
would be granted to a far wider community. It is the universal
testimony of the New Testament that this day has come in and
through Jesus. Especially does Luke set out to indicate step by
step the difficulties and obstructions which stand in the way
of a truly universal gospel. But in Luke's eyes the outcome is
never doubted: God's Spirit will withstand any barrier and
constructs.

What, then, is glossolalia in the context of Acts? It is the effort to express the inexpressible: the indwelling of the Spirit of
God in the lives of men. When the kerygma sank home to a
responsive heart, ordinary human language could not express
the emotions that were aroused; therefore, the believer broke
forth in ecstatic speech. These may have been words and/or

---

[132]L. S. Thornton, *The Common Life in the Body of Christ* (4th ed.;
Dacre Press, 1963), pp. 37ff.

[133]Cf. Hebrews 3:14 and 6:4.

phrases, such as "Jesus is Lord" (1 Cor. 12:3); or "Abba, Father" (Rom 8:15-16; Gal. 3:6). Other sounds were not recognizable as words at all. At times a continuous, elevated discourse was discernible, perhaps giving the impression that it might be a foreign language. At other times there was an inward groaning and sighs too deep for words (Rom. 8:26).

But it is not sufficient to write off these phenomena as mere gibberish or incoherent nonsense. The speaker was not "out of control." Neither was he in an emotional debauch. Rather, for the believer these manifestations indicated the overwhelming power and presence of the Spirit of God in his life.

In the light of Luke's theological interests—the Spirit of God as power—it is now possible to examine the remaining two references to glossolalia in Acts.

TONGUES AT CAESAREA AND EPHESUS

> While Peter was still saying this, the Holy Spirit fell on all who heard the word. And the believers from among the circumcised who came with Peter were amazed, because the gift of the Holy Spirit had been poured out even on the Gentiles. For they had heard them speaking in tongues and extolling God (Acts 10:44-46a).

If Philip's mission may be termed a "Samaritan Pentecost," then this incident may well be termed a "Gentile Pentecost."[134] Luke presents Peter as having received instructions from the Spirit (Acts 10:19) to go to Cornelius. Peter reluctantly proclaimed to him the good news; and while the apostle was still preaching, the Holy Spirit "fell" on all who heard the word and produced in them the effects of Pentecost, i.e., glossolalia. Probably because the case involving Cornelius is unique, Luke dwells upon it at such length, relating the account twice (cf. Acts 11). Luke is careful to indicate clearly that this gentile convert received the Spirit in exactly the same manner as did the

---

[134]Dewar, *The Holy Spirit and Modern Thought*, p. 54.

Jewish disciples at Pentecost. It is important to note, then, that the glossolalia occurs in a context where the gospel is breaking through the "gentile" barrier. Peter earnestly asks, in view of what happened: "Can anyone forbid water for baptizing these people who have received the Holy Spirit just as we have?" (Acts 10:47). The Greek infinitive κωλῦσαι translated "forbid" corresponds to the adverb ἀκωλύτως with which Luke strangely ends his book. Frank Stagg[135] builds a convincing case around this "unhindered" motif, and he sees in it the basic theological message of Acts, i.e., that Luke's writing describes the hard-won liberty of the gospel as it broke down human barriers of separatism and isolation. Luke, then, may well have viewed this instance of glossolalia as another manifestation of the outpouring of the Holy Spirit, paralleling for these "God-fearers" the Pentecost event.

When Peter returned to Jerusalem he had to relate the entire story point by point in order to clear the air, for there was great conflict in the church concerning the relationship of the gospel to the gentiles. Was this new religion of Jesus for the gentiles as well as the Jews? The simple fact was that *God had come to the house of Cornelius*; the Holy Spirit had fallen upon them just as upon the apostles at Pentecost. Glossolalia was an important link in this affirmation, since it had likewise been manifested earlier. There was no valid argument that could be lodged in light of what had happened: the tongues experience was evidence that God's Spirit had overturned Jewish particularism and opened the church to the gentiles.

Similarly, the incident of glossolalia at Ephesus was Luke's way of indicating that God's approval rested upon the experience of the people there. Ephesus was known as a center of Greek and pagan culture,[136] and Luke saw the gospel's penetration there as but another evidence of the Spirit's shattering of the barrier of Jewish particularism.

---

[135]Stagg, op. cit., pp. 1-17, 120.

[136]John P. Newport, "Speaking with Tongues," *Home Missions*, 36 (May 1965): 9.

> And Paul said, "John baptized with the baptism of repen-
> tance, telling the people to believe in the one who was to come
> after him, that is, Jesus." On hearing this, they were baptized
> in the name of the Lord Jesus. And when Paul had laid his
> hands upon them, the Holy Spirit came on them; and they
> spoke with tongues and prophesied (Acts 19:4-6).

Malcolm Tolbert maintains, with many other scholars, that
one of the obvious, primary emphases of Luke-Acts was to
demonstrate that the inclusion of "the gentiles in the Christian
movement was inherent in the Old Testament, intended by the
founder of Christianity, and proceeded under the direction of
God."[137]

The special manifestations of the presence of the Spirit
come at crucial points in early Christian development: at Pentecost for the Jews, at the conversion of the Samaritans, upon
God-fearing Greeks at Caesarea, and now in the winning of
these followers of John the Baptist.

Step by step, then, Luke is intent on showing that it was
God—through his Spirit—that impelled men to take the gospel to non-Jews. It was He who validated their efforts by pour-
ing out the Holy Spirit on the new converts who would not
have been accepted readily as Christians without some "sign"
of God's presence in their lives.

> New Samaritan Christians received the Holy Spirit as evi-
> dence of the genuineness of their conversion. An angel of the
> Lord guided Philip to the Ethiopian eunuch. In spite of Peter's
> reluctance God literally compelled him to carry the gospel to
> Cornelius. The Holy Spirit led the church in Antioch to initi-
> ate a mission to Gentiles. Finally, God led Paul to Macedonia

---

[137]Malcolm Tolbert, "Leading Ideas of the Gospel of Luke," *Review and Expositor*, 64 (Fall 1967): 444. The existence of at least some
of the documents which underlie Luke's gospel makes it possible for
scholars to draw with some degree of accuracy certain conclusions
concerning the theological posture of Luke.

after he was prevented by the Holy Spirit from beginning work in Asia Minor.[138]

Luke was intent, then, on showing how the various barriers were broken down between Jews, Samaritans, and gentiles. He indicates the presence of God's Spirit at each "crossing."

> Pentecost does not stand alone in Acts; it is to be seen along with the giving of the Spirit to others as to Jews: to Samaritans (8:17), in the reaching of the Ethiopian eunuch, a "God-fearing Greek" (8:29, 39), in the winning of Cornelius, another "God-fearing Greek" (10:44-47, 11:15), and to former followers of John the Baptist who had not followed Christ (19:6).[139]

It is no accident that the gift of tongues is traced to the Holy Spirit in Acts 2:4, 10:46, 19:6. It was for Luke a phenomenon which legitimately validated the presence of the Spirit of God. Luke would not intend the Christians of subsequent generations should formalize the experience into a kind of religious panacea, far superior to any other manifestation of possession by God's Spirit.

CONCLUSION

Glossolalia in Acts obviously can be understood only through the eyes of the author. In light of the emphasis placed upon the role of the Spirit in the early Christian community, and in light of Luke's approach to the problem of Jewish isolationism, glossolalia should be seen as *a* legitimate example of the way God worked through these Christian pioneers to the end that all men might come into the circle of the redeemed. The phenomenon is an objective manifestation of the power of God's Spirit as it "filled" these Christians, giving them the requisite power for their mission.

---

[138]Tolbert, op. cit., p. 445.

[139]Frank Stagg, "The Holy Spirit in the New Testament," *Review and Expositor*, 63 (Spring 1966): 139.

4

GLOSSOLALIA
IN 1 CORINTHIANS

From the outset the ambivalence of the apostle Paul concerning glossolalia is apparent:

> I thank God that I speak in tongues more than you all; nevertheless, in church I would rather speak five words with my mind, in order to instruct others, than ten thousand words in a tongue (1 Cor. 14:18-19).

The result of this statement is two-fold: on the one hand, the glossolalist groups find it salutary that Paul can be counted in their number;[1] on the other hand, non-glossolalists focus upon the latter half of the statement and stress Paul's disap-

---

[1]For example see William G. MacDonald, *Glossolalia in the New Testament* (Gospel Publishing House, n.d.), p. 20, who notes that "his [Paul's] 'command of the Lord'—*do not forbid glossolalia*, but do all things properly and in order—has never been revoked!"

proval.[2] What could account for this apparent ambivalent attitude on the part of Paul toward glossolalia? It is to this and other questions that this chapter turns.

PAUL AND CORINTH

The Corinth which Paul knew was a "young" city of about one hundred years. The original (and ancient[3]) Corinth had been destroyed by the Romans in 146 B.C., and it had lain in waste until Julius Caesar rebuilt the city in 46 B.C.[4] During the next hundred years Corinth prospered and flourished as an important commercial city.

Situated fifty miles due west of Athens, Corinth was the political and commercial capital of the Roman province of Achaia to which most of Greece and Macedonia belonged. Strategically located, it lay upon a strip of land which con-

---

[2]For example see Charles William Shumway, "A Critical History of Glossolalia" (unpublished doctor's dissertation, Boston University, 1919), p. 10, who concedes that Paul said, "Forbid not to speak in tongues." He notes further, however, that "we believe the exhortation was based more largely upon any sympathy with the glossolalia as exhibited at Corinth." Cf. J. P. M. Sweet, "A Sign for Unbelievers: Paul's Attitude to Glossolalia," *New Testament Studies*, 13 (April 1967): 240 and Elias Andrews, "Tongues, Gift Of," *The Interpreter's Dictionary of the Bible*, George Authur Buttrick, editor (4 vols.; Abingdon Press, 1962), R-Z: 672.

[3]Before 146 B.C. its name had been Ephyra, meaning "lookout." After 46 B.C. it was called Colonia Laus Julia Corinthiensis. Jack Finegan, "Corinth," *The Interpreter's Dictionary of the Bible*, George Arthur Buttrick, editor (4 vols.; Abingdon Press, 1962), A-D: 682. Cf. Maurice Holleaux, *Etudes d'Epigraphie et d'Historie Greeques* (3 vols.; E. de Boccard, 1938-1942), 1:65ff.

[4]Rhys Carpenter, *Ancient Corinth* (American School of Classical Studies, 1954), p. 13. Excavations have been conducted at Corinth since 1896. See Rhys Carpenter, *Ancient Corinth: A Guide to Excavations* (2nd. ed.; American School of Classical Studies, 1933) and Finegan, op. cit., pp. 682-84.

nected the Peloponnesian peninsula with the mainland. It was virtually a "land-bridge" across which all northern and southern traffic passed. This unique geographical feature had even greater prominence in that in the first century many ships were hauled across the tiny strip of land on specially built tracks, thus avoiding several days at sea. Corinth, then, was literally a crossroads of sea traffic between east and west, Asia and Europe.

Corinth was naturally a hub of business activity. At the very center of the city stood the *agora*, or market place. Various kinds of shops lined the streets. The diverse business places unearthed by archaeologists indicate that the city was functionally a commercial one.[5] The famed Isthmian games occasioned a national festival which brought throngs of people into the city and boosted significantly Corinth's "tourist-trade."[6]

Since the time of Aristophanes the term κορινθιάζεσθαι had been a synonym for drunken and immoral debauchery.[7] "To live like a Corinthian" was by the first century a hackneyed expression for dissolute living. The teeming multitudes which flooded Corinth brought with them many customs and crudities, their gods as well as their godlessness. At Corinth archaeologists have uncovered remains of temples to the Egyptian divinities Isis and Serapis, to the Phrygian goddess Magna Mater, to the Syrian deity Astarte, and the Ephesian

---

[5]G. Ernest Wright, *Biblical Archaeology* (The Westminster Press, 1960), pp. 175-78. Cf. Ferdinand J. de Weale, "The Roman Market North of the Temple at Corinth," *American Journal of Archaeology*, 34 (1930): 432-54; Oscar Broneer, "Excavations in the Agora at Corinth," *American Journal of Archeology*, 37 (1933): 554-72; Henry J. Cadbury, "The Macellum of Corinth," *Journal of Biblical Literature*, 53 (1934): 134-41.

[6]Paul refers to "race" and "corruptible crown" in 1 Corinthians 9:24-27. Thus, he had some knowledge of the games. See Oscar Broneer, "Corinth," *The Biblical Archaeologist*, 14 (December 1951): 82.

[7]John Taylor Dean, *St. Paul and Corinth* (Lutterworth Press, 1947), p. 15.

Artemis and Aphrodite.[8] The temple of Aphrodite, the goddess of love and lust, is credited by Strabo[9] as having a thousand priestess-prostitutes attached to it.[10] Strabo further observes:

> It was on account of these women that the city was crowded with people and grew rich; for instance, the ship captains freely squandered their money, and hence the proverb, 'Not for every man is the voyage to Corinth.'[11]

The influx of foreign peoples who are themselves devotees to the mysteries, linked with the social complexities of any cosmopolitan area, combined to make Corinth a hotbed of vice and corruption. In addition to the crude and base sins, there were active in Corinth more recondite vices brought in by the seamen and traders from the four corners of the Mediterranean world. By the time Paul came to Corinth the term was not only a synonym for drunkenness and debauchery, but also for filth itself. As Joseph Callaway has summarized, "Corinth was in no 'Bible Belt.' "[12]

Yet into such a social climate Paul addresses one of his most eloquent writings. 1 Corinthians 12-14 ranks among the finest texts in the New Testament. 1 Corinthians 12:1 begins a detailed discussion περὶ τῶν πνευματικῶν. This discussion stretches through three chapters. His is a plea for love, the noblest gift of the Spirit. This gift has as its goal rational

---

[8]See Broneer, "Corinth," pp. 83-88 for a discussion of myths associated with Corinth.

[9]Quoted in ibid., p. 88. Cf. William A. McDonald, "Corinth," *Biblical Archaeologist*, 5 (September 1942): 46.

[10]Strabo, *Geography*, VIII, vi, 20 in Horace Leonard Jones (trans.), *The Geography of Strabo*, "The Loeb Classical Library" (8 vols.; William Heinemann, 1927-1932), 4:189-91.

[11]Ibid., pp. 189-93.

[12]Joseph A. Callaway, "Corinth," *Review and Expositor*, 57 (October 1960): 384.

preaching which is in sharp contrast to the glossolalia which is causing dissension and individualism at Corinth. The contents of these chapters reveal that Paul had a deeper knowledge of the problem of glossolalia at Corinth than a simple inquiry would afford him.[13]

Paul speaks as though he were sure of the situation he addressed, and his confidence implies that he had information descriptive of the glossolalia at Corinth. The source of what Paul knew is impossible to determine. Clearly he knew the manner of worship that the Corinthians came to use during the first visit to Corinth. Comments by the bearers of the letter from Corinth or by "those of Chloe" may have brought him up to date on this aspect of the Corinthians' worship.

In discussing spiritual gifts Paul devotes chapter 14 to an examination of glossolalia and its interpretation and to prophecy. The three chapters are inextricably bound together.

Paul begins his discussion of spiritual gifts by differentiating between Christian experience and pagan worship. The pagan gods are idols that must be carefully distinguished from the Spirit of God. Paul specifically mentions, as a *charisma*, the gift of distinguishing between spirits; therefore in Paul's mind the gift of discernment would enable one to determine whether glossolalia was spoken by the Spirit of God or was demonic in origin.

1 Corinthians includes two lists of some of the spiritual gifts. Included among those listed twice are the discernment of spirits, prophecy, kinds of tongues, and the interpretation of tongues (1 Cor. 12:8-10, 12:28-30). Although Paul's whole ar-

---

[13]It is, in fact, difficult to know with certainty whether this section was occasioned by a question from the Corinthian Church. Cf. Archibald Robertson and Alfred Plummer, *A Critical and Exegetical Commentary on the First Epistle of St. Paul to the Corinthians* (2nd ed.; Charles Scribner's Sons, 1925), p. 257, who note: "There is a possible reference to the letter of the Corinthians to the Apostle; but he would no doubt have treated a number of the topics which are handled, even if they had not mentioned them."

gument emphasizes that no one gift is superior to another in the body of Christ, it is interesting that in both lists he places "kinds of tongues" and "interpretation of tongues" *last*. Chapter 13 does begin with a reference to tongues, and it is *first* in the list; however, in this instance the gifts seem to increase in value as enumerated rather than to decrease.

Of these three chapters which deal with spiritual gifts, it is chapter 14 which contains the discussion of glossolalia. Inevitably the sense of the Greek is obscured in the English translation. The King James Version, for example, interpolated the word "unknown," thereby conveying the idea of foreign language.[14] Edgar Goodspeed paraphrased "speaking in tongues" with "speak ecstatically."[15]

Finally, it is helpful to bear in mind that Paul does not present a thorough, descriptive analysis of the nature and value of glossolalia; on the contrary, he is intent to deal pastorally with the problem in Corinth since the "spiritual ones" have over-emphasized glossolalia to the neglect of prophecy in the vernacular.

THE HISTORY OF THE INTERPRETATION OF GLOSSOLALIA AT CORINTH

Background of Glossolalia at Corinth

Varied cultures, races, religions and philosophies mingled at Corinth. Pausanias' vivid description of the multiplicity of temples and religious statues is most impressive.[16] Since the

---

[14]See King James Version, 1 Corinthians 14:4, 14:13, 14:14, 14:19, 14:27.

[15]Edgar J. Goodspeed (trans.), *New Testament: An American Translation* (University of Chicago Press, 1923), p. 331.

[16]Pausanias, *Description of Greece*, II, 27 in W. H. S. Jones (trans.), *Pausanias, Description of Greece*. "The Loeb Classical Library" (5 vols.; Harvard University Press, 1918-1935), 1:333-37. Cf. Jane Harrison, *Prolegomena to the Study of Greek Religion* (Meridian Books, 1955), pp. 363ff., 478ff. and L. R. Farnell, *The Higher Aspects of Greek Religion* (Williams and Morgate, 1912), passim.

Christians in Corinth were converts from Judaism and paganism, the background of rivalry was potentially dangerous to the Corinthian church.[17] Rudolf Bultmann assumes that Paul's discussion of tongues was in answer to the question: "By what criterion can divine and demonic ecstasy be distinguished from each other?"[18] Quite possibly the debate in Corinth concerning spiritual gifts, especially tongues, had built up to a point where serious division threatened the fellowship, the worship, and above all, the missionary enterprise.

Many scholars follow a line similar to that taken by Walter Baür, W. F. Arndt and F. W. Gingrich. These lexicographers suggest that

> there is no doubt about the thing referred to, namely the broken speech of persons in religious ecstasy. The phenomenon, as found in Hellenistic religion, is described by . . . E. Rohde and Reitzenstein.[19]

This assumption, i.e., that glossolalia at Corinth is similar to the ecstatic utterances of the Hellenistic religions, is accepted

---

[17] The poorly cut inscription, "Synagogue of the Hebrews," found at Corinth, indicates that the Jews there were not a strong group. Cf. Finegan, op. cit., p. 684. See also Jack Finegan, *Light from the Ancient Past* (Princeton University Press, 1946), p. 362.

[18] Rudolf Bultmann, *Theology of the New Testament*, trans. Kendrick Grobel (2 vols.; SCM Press, 1965), 1:163-64.

[19] Walter Baür, *A Greek-English Lexicon of the New Testament and Other Early Christian Literature*, trans. William F. Arndt and F. Wilbur Gingrich (4th rev. ed.; University of Chicago Press, 1952), p. 161. Arndt and Gingrich are referring to Edwin Rohde, *Psyche* (Harcourt, Brace and Company, 1925) and Richard Reitzenstein, *Poimandres: Studien zur griechisch griechisch-ägyptischen und frühchristlichen Literatur* (B. G. Teubner, 1904).

by many notable scholars.[20] The following section proposes to examine the relationship between the tongues at Corinth and the ecstaticism of Hellenistic religion.

Examples of ecstaticism in Hellenistic religion. Those who would understand the origin of glossolalia in terms of Hellenistic religions cite several "examples" of parallel phenomena.

In terms of gnosticism, the mention of "the Powers, who are above the substance of the eighth sphere, singing praise to God with a voice (φωνή) that is theirs alone,"[21] is not really germane since it is probably not earlier than the third century A.D.; furthermore, its point of origin is likely to be Egypt.

The most famous of all the ecstatic prophets of Greece was the Pythia at Delphi, who is Plato's first example of prophetic madness in the *Phaedras*.[22] E. R. Dodds hold that prophetic madness is at least as old in Greece as the religion of Apollo.[23]

---

[20]Cf. Héring, op. cit., p. 128; Andrews, op. cit., p. 671; James Moffatt, *The First Epistle of Paul to the Corinthians* (Harper and Brothers, 1933), pp. 207-708; Johannes Behm, "γλῶσσα," *Theological Dictionary of the New Testament*, Gerhard Kittel, editor; trans. Geoffrey W. Bromiley (10 vols.; Eerdmans, 1964-1976), 1:719-27; Maurice Barnett, *The Living Flame* (Epworth Press, 1953), pp. 102-103; Clarence T. Craig, "Exegesis: The First Epistle to the Corinthians," *The Interpreter's Bible*, George Arthur Buttrick, editor (12 vols.; Abingdon Press, 1953), 10:146.

[21]*Corpus Hermeticium*, I, 26a in Walter Scott, *Mernetica* (4 vols.; Clarendon Press, 1924-1936), 1:129.

[22]Rohde, op. cit., p. 289, feels that Plato is wrong in ascribing prophetic madness to Apollonian religion which was "hostile to anything in the nature of ecstasy." B. R. Dodds, *The Greeks and the Irrational* (Beacon Press, 1951), p. 69, contends that Rohde is wrong.

[23]Dodds, op. cit., pp. 70-71. Kurt Latte, "The Coming of the Pythia," *The Harvard Theological Review*, 33 (1940): 9-18, points out that the term "ecstasy" is fluid and can denote either a strong agitation of the body or a relative passivity of the body. "There is no doubt that the state of the Pythia resembled the second rather than the first." Ibid., p. 12.

Apollo used "enthusiasm" in its original and literal sense with the Pythia at Delphi. The god entered into her and used her vocal organs as if they were his own. He spoke through her in the first person, not the third.[24] Before the inquirer entered the temple, the Pythia was already under the influence of Apollo and was in some abnormal state of trance or ecstasy. The chief priest would ask the inquirer's question. The Pythia's answer would vary in its degree of coherence and intelligibility. When it had been given, the chief priest would dictate it to the inquirer. Thus,

> the exact words of the Pythia cannot be taken to be recorded in our authorities. They give at best the authentic text of the oracle as delivered in its definitive version by the prophet to the inquirer.[25]

Since it is impossible to know the exact nature of the speech of the Pythia, an examination of the nature of her inspiration is the only course open to scholarship in seeking to see her relationship to glossolalia. The most reliable description of the psychological state of the Pythia comes from Plutarch, who possibly received the information first hand from the prophet Nicander. While the incident he relates was certainly an exceptional occurrence, it does reveal some important features of the ecstatic prophetesses at Delphi.

> Whenever, then, the imaginative and prophetic faculty is in a state of proper adjustment for attempering itself to the spirit as to a drug, inspiration in those who foretell the future is bound to come; and whenever the conditions are not thus, it is bound not to come, or when it does come to be misleading, abnormal and confusing, as we know in the case of the priestess who died not so long ago. As it happened, a deputation from abroad had arrived to consult the oracle. The victim (i.e., the goat to be sacrificed), it is said, remained unmoved

---

[24]Dodds, loc. cit.

[25]H. W. Parke and D. E. W. Wormell, *The Delphic Oracle* (2 vols.; Blackwell, 1956), 1:33.

and unaffected in any way by the first libations; but the priests, in their eagerness to please, went far beyond their wonted usage, and only after the victim had been subjected to a deluge and nearly drowned did at last give in (i.e., shiver). What then, was the result touching the priestess? She went down into the oracle unwillingly, they say, and half-heartedly; and at her first responses it was at once plain from the harshness of her voice that she was not responding properly; she was like a labouring ship and was filled with a mighty and baleful spirit. Finally she became hysterical and with a frightful shriek rushed towards the exit and threw herself down, with the result that not only the members of the deputation fled, but also the oracle interpreter Nicander and those holy men that were present. However, after a little, they went in and took her up, still conscious; and she lived on for a few days.[26]

This account indicates that the trance or ecstasy was still genuine in Plutarch's time. This "change" in the voice is mentioned elsewhere in Plutarch as a common feature of "enthusiasm."[27] Though the evidence is lacking, it appears that her inspiration was due to "possession." Further, it is interesting to note that, though the oracles used a physical means to induce the state of inspiration, as did the mysteries, there was a great deal of difference in the purpose and result of their efforts and the frenzied confusion of the mysteries. The purpose of the former was evidently to gain some *knowledge* from the god; the latter sought to achieve *union* with the god.

Third example of Plato,[28] the Sibyl, also belongs to the group of ecstatic prophets of the pagan world; therefore, some

---

[26]Plutarch, *Obsolescence of Oracles*, 438, 51 in Frank Cole Babbitt (trans.), *Plutarch's Moralia*. "The Loeb Classical Library" (10 vols.; William Heinemann, 1944-1949), 5:499.

[27]Dodds, op. cit., p. 73, citing Plutarch.

[28]Plato's second example of prophetic madness is that of the priestesses of Dodona. This oracle, however, has more of the divination type, since the priestesses interpreted the rustling of the leaves in an oak. No one suggests that glossolalia was manifested here. Cf. J. E. Pontenrose, "Dodona," *The Oxford Classical Dictionary* (Clarendon Press, 1949), p. 294a.

scholars allege that she manifested glossolalia.[29] The first mention of the Sibyl is in Heraclitus. He notes that "the Sibyl with raving voice speaks words that have no part in laughter or in rich apparel or in unguents. Yet she prevails; for it is the god who drives her."[30] Her oracles were composed in verse. Cicero noted that they were frequently composed with an acrostic, so that the first letter of each verse taken in order conveyed a meaning.[31] Just as at Delphi, interpreters were needed. Émile Lombard contends that since the interpreters were needed, the original speech must have been unintelligible.[32] Just the opposite could be true, however, in light of the tremendous respect, honor and awe which the Sibyl evidently commanded. That is, the inquirer would want words of Sibyl and not those of an inquirer.

To summarize, aside from the possibility of unintelligible speech, the other characteristics of Sibyl, i.e., ecstatic trance, loss of consciousness, change of voice, can be accounted for in terms of the concept of spirit possession in the ancient world.

Finally, Dionysus (Bacchus) originated either in Thrace or Phyrgia. The aim of the cult was apparently a cathartic experience produced music. By a whirling dance, and, sometimes, by intoxication. Due to the ecstasy, loss of consciousness, and

---

[29]"Tongues, Gift of," The Encyclopaedia Britannica (23 vols.; William Benton, 1962), 22:288. Cf. Ira J. Martin, Glossolalia in the Apostolic Church: A Survey in Tongue Speech (Berea College Press, 1960), p. 78.

[30]Fragment 92 in Hermann Diels, Die Fragmente der Versokratiker (2 vols.; Weidmann, 1951-1952), 1:94.

[31]Cicero, De Divinatione, II, 54 in William A. Balconer (trans.), Cicero. "The Loeb Classical Library" (William Heinemann, 1946), 497.

[32]Émile Lombard, De la Glossolalie chez les premiers Chrétiens (Bridel, 1910), pp. 93-94.

possession by the deity, there was also some ecstatic prophecy, though this seemed to play a minor role.

Similarities. First, it is apparent that the Pythia at Delphi demonstrated divine madness or ecstasy. The reaction of detached spectators is similar to that reflected in the Corinthian letter when Paul indicates that outsiders might consider the participants mad.[33] Second, disorder and confusion seem to have been evident in both the Corinthian worship and among the pagan rites cited above.[34] Finally, the use of intoxication in the Bacchic revelries parallels the criticism of some of the onlookers at Pentecost that "they [the disciples] are filled with new wine."[35]

Differences. The significance of the ecstatic state is different in Paul from the mysteries, Plato and the oracles. In these latter instances the emphasis was upon learning the "secrets" of the gods; in the former the theoretical end was meaningful communion (but not union) with God who had bestowed this gift of the Holy Spirit. Also, it is significant that Paul consistently maintained distinction between tongues and prophecy, a distinction which did not exist in the other pagan rites.

In Paul's exhortation to the Ephesians, "Do not get drunk with wine, for that is debauchery, but be filled with the Spirit,"[36] the relationship of inebriation and inspiration to that of the intoxication in the Bacchic revelries is that of opposition

---

[33]Cf. the charge that "they are filled with new wine" in Acts 2:13b.

[34]Strabo, *Geography*, X, iii, 13, 16 in Horace Jones, op. cit., 5:99-101, gives an account of the whirling of symbols and clanging of castanets that were used in the worship of Dionysus and Cybele. Barnett, op. cit., pp. 101-102, suggests that this might well be in the background of Paul's condemnation of "the sounding brass and tinkling symbol" in 1 Corinthians 13:1.

[35]Acts 16:16. Cf. Ephesians 5:18: "And do not get drunk with wine, for that is debauchery; but be filled with the Spirit."

[36]Ephesians 5:18.

and not agreement, showing only outward similarity.[37] In the Bacchic rites the ecstatic experience was sought after per se, and furthermore, it was induced by artificial means. The New Testament does not betray such artificiality. The infilling of the Holy Spirit comes without psychological inducements. The Spirit-filled person remains in full control of his gifts.[38] Again, the oracles were consulted for information known only to the gods, and the prophetess did not speak voluntarily. Those who interpreted these oracles took the initiative in posing the questions to the oracle, and often their "interpretation" was as vague as the oracle itself. In Paul, it is Christ who approaches the believer.

In the Hellenistic religions, there appears to be a loss of self-control in the ecstatic state. Paul, however, presupposes that the believers at Corinth should control the gift of tongues. In fact, he offers certain specific suggestions to aid in achieving a degree of orderliness.

Finally, the ethical implications mark the most apparent difference. In paganism there is no parallel to the teaching of Paul in 1 Corinthians that the Spirit ministers love within the congregation. Paul definitely attributed ethical conduct to the work of the Spirit (Rom. 8:4-9). Bultmann concludes:

> The really characteristic feature of his [Paul's] conception of the Spirit, however, is the fact that he reckons the ministrations of love within the congregation among the Spirit's workings, an idea evidently foreign to the popular view, . . . and the futher fact that he attributes ethical conduct to the Spirit.[39]

Conclusion. While there likely is a certain formal, external connection between the ecstaticism of certain pagan religious practices and glossolalia, the phenomenon about which Paul wrote in 1 Corinthians 14, when rightly understood and prac-

---

[37]Lombard, op. cit., p. 92.

[38]Barnett, op. cit., p. 104. Cf. 1 Corinthians 14:32-33, 14:39-40.

[39]Bultmann, op. cit., p. 337.

ticed, does not signify identical concepts as those for which certain ecstatic phenomena stood. It is fallacious to argue that, because of certain parallelisms, Corinthian glossolalia at its deepest level betrayed the same meaning as the wild, ecstatic frenzies of the Hellenistic religions. That its *form* bore some semblance to these phenomena is most probable, however.

It will be necessary to look elsewhere in order to discover the origin of glossolalia at Corinth.

Background of Glossolalia in the Psyche of Mankind

Although glossolalia is a religious phenomenon, it "can be studied empirically from a socio-psychological point of view."[40] Due to the danger, however, of allowing psychological explanations to dictate the use of the biblical evidence, this chapter has begun with a discussion of the possible antecedents to glossolalia as well as an exposition of the primary biblical occurrences in Acts, rather than with psychological theories themselves.[41] Nevertheless, much is to be learned concerning the phenomenon from a psychological perspective, and it cannot be denied that many scholars see the origin of glossolalia not peculiar to Corinth—or to biblical history—but representative of the psychological constituent of mankind, which is a factor present in every age. Although this chapter is not psychologically oriented, brief attention will now be given to the more prominent theories of this nature.

Glossolalia as psychopathic phenomena. Since the time of William James, who suggested that a psychopathic temperament was often present in religious leaders, students of psychology of religion have not hesitated to consider the possibility of psy-

---

[40]Wayne E. Oates, "A Socio-Psychological Study of Glossolalia," in Frank Stagg, E. Glenn Hinson and Wayne E. Oates, *Glossolalia: Tongue Speaking in Biblical, Historical, and Psychological Perspective* (Abingdon Press, 1967), p. 76.

[41]For additional citations, see "bibliography" below.

chopathic involvement in religious experience.[42] Though encountered rather infrequently, one explanation of glossolalia is to regard it simply as a case of hysteria.[43] Medically, hysteria may be defined as

> a psychoneurosis, the symptoms of which are based on conversion and which is characterized by lack of control over acts and emotions, by morbid self-consciousness, by anxiety, by exaggeration of the effect of sensory impressions, and by stimulation of various disorders.[44]

Thus, hysteria is a neurological disorder which is not organic but functional in origin.

The most comprehensive book in the English-speaking world which deals with glossolalia from a psychological point of view is the work by George Cutten.[45] He classifies glossolalia as a religious experience which has similar symptoms to allied phenomena like hysteria and catalepsy. He shows, for example, that the hysteric, like the glossolalic, is most susceptible to suggestion, manifests exaggerated sensations, and betrays weird bodily contortions during his periods of rapture.

On the other hand, it is important to note that while hysteria used to be a common occurrence, especially among women, genuine cases of hysteria in recent years are increasingly difficult to isolate.[46] Also, it is significant that, judging from the extant materials from the apostolic period, glosso-

---

[42]William James, *The Varieties of Religious Experience* (Longmans, Green, and Company, 1902), pp. 23, 478.

[43]Ibid., p. 413. Cf. George B. Cutten, *Speaking with Tongues: Historically and Psychologically Considered* (Yale University Press, 1927), p. 158.

[44]W. A. Newman Dorland, *The American Illustrated Medical Dictionary* (21st. ed.; W. B. Saunders Company, 1947), p. 702.

[45]Cutten, op. cit., passim.

[46]Carney Landis and Marjorie M. Bolles, *Textbook of Abnormal Psychology* (Macmillan and Company, 1946), p. 94.

lalia was predominantly a masculine phenomenon, not femi-
nine.[47] Cutten observes that "in all forms of nervous
instability females predominate, and in hysteria they are in
the proportion of twenty females to one male."[48]

   Glossolalia as ecstaticism and related phenomenon. It is much
more common in psychological circles to explain glossolalia as
a manifestation of ecstasy[49] in which verbal automatisms are
expressed from the unconscious.[50] Lombard notes that

> in terms more directly borrowed from the vocabulary of mod-
> ern psychology, we are concerned with a state of personal dis-
> aggregation, in which the speech-motor center of the subject
> obeys subconscious impulses. The glossolalia is an *automatic*
> phenomenon, which signifies only that it be loosed of all vol-
> untary and cognate character; *automatic* means here, foreign
> to the conscious "Ego" being a modality and a part of the total
> "I."[51]

Eddison Mosiman has likened glossolalia to a state of hypnosis.[52] He points to the parallels between the conditions used to
produce a hypnotic state and those exhibited by the glossolalist: fixation of attention, uniformity of perception, limitation

---

[47]Martin, op. cit., p. 97.

[48]Cutten, op. cit., p. 159. A second pathological explanation
which has been made is a partially developed catalepsy. This illness
is characterized by suspension of sensation, the loss of consciousness, the deprivation of volition, the presence of delirium, etc. Cf.
Anton T. Boisen, *Religion in Crisis and Custom: A Sociological and Psychological Study* (Harper and Brothers, 1955), p. 78.

[49]See above, chapter 2.

[50]George Albert Coe, *The Psychology of Religion* (University of Chicago Press, 1916), pp. 185, 194.

[51]Lombard, op. cit., p. 6.

[52]Eddison Mosiman, *Das Zungenreden geschichtlich und psychologisch untersucht* (J. C. B. Mohr, 1911), p. 109.

of the power of the will, and suppression of ideas.[53] Cutten criticizes this position because he feels that it carries the importance of auto-suggestion too far.[54] Aside from terminology it appears, however, that Mosiman agrees with Lombard. Mosiman observes that

> the essence of the pyschological explanation of speaking with tongues is an utterance of thought and feeling through the speech organ, which temporarily is under the control of the reflexive nerve center, and the special forms are primarily attributed to the suggestion which mainly arises out of a literal understanding of the New Testament.[55]

Ira J. Martin understands glossolalia "to be an ecstatic form of speech, seeking to give vent to the joy of the new life of spiritual redemption."[56] He concludes that glossolalia is one form of psychic catharsis, "a genuine but not universal concomitant of the Christian conversion experience."[57] Furthermore, Martin differentiates two types of glossolalia: the genuine and the synthetic. The former represents a "psychic catharsis."

> In the deep basic reintegration of the individual's personality, the psychological unheaval is too great to control: the resultant joy of the release from guilt-feeling is too thrilling to repress, and the eager desire to express one's new life of inner peace and fresh outlook cannot be restrained.[58]

Synthetic glossolalia represents that glossolalia which occurs

---

[53]Cited in Cutten, op. cit., p. 166.

[54]Ibid., pp. 165-66. Cf. Martin, op. cit., pp. 97-98.

[55]Mosiman, op. cit., p. 114.

[56]Martin, *Glossolalia in the Apostolic Church*, p. 100.

[57]Ibid.

[58]Ibid.

when other factors are operating, e.g., auto-hypnosis, normal hypnosis and auto-suggestion.[59]

Lombard suggests a three-fold classification of "automatic speech."[60] These "types" represent degrees of progression from the remote forms to the nearer and more familiar forms of organized language. First, there are inarticulate sounds such as hiccups, cries, sighs, wailings and murmurs. These simple, vocal sounds are especially apparent in glossolalists at the beginning of their automatism. The second classification encompasses the most common type of glossolalia, a pseudo-language or speech composed of articulate sounds which resemble words. There is actually a phonic differentiation, and the person *seems* to be speaking and expressing definite ideas. In reality, however, the language itself is meaningless and has no content. Finally, there are "manufactured" or "coined" words (neologisms) which emerge upon a base of well-characterized pseudo-language and have a constant representative value or meaning.

There is little doubt that such ecstatic speech could and does still persist in modern times. The difficulty arises, however, from the fact that these explanations do not coincide with the biblical data. Taken at face value the biblical text indicates that Paul confronts a glossolalia which *could be interpreted*, while Luke seems to indicate a polyglottism which was recognized by dispersion Jews as their native language. Thus, to consider that tongue-speaking was only an ecstatic automatism requires a revision of the biblical evidence.

Glossolalia as unconscious memory. The previous discussions have viewed the glossolalia as a meaningless language. A third approach regards the glossolalia as real foreign

---

[59]Andrew D. Lester, "Glossolalia: A Psychological Evaluation" (unpublished seminar paper, Southern Baptist Theological Seminary, 1965), p. 10.

[60]Lombard, op. cit., pp. 25-34. This classification is also followed by Cutten, op. cit., pp. 169-76.

languages[61] uttered from the unconscious memory of an individual, which is not consciously known. The memory is able to store all impressions that enter it. The aging William Cullen Bryant said that if he were given a few moments for reflection he could recite any line he had ever written.[62] Memory deposits supposedly long forgotten, or even so fully forgotten that there is no memory that they ever existed at all, have been recalled.[63] Arthur Wright was perhaps the first in the period of modern psychology to offer this explanation of glossolalia.[64] Both Jerusalem and Corinth were cosmopolitan areas—as were Ephesus and Caesarea—and the glossolalia could be words and phrases of many different languages "stored" unconsciously in the memory of the speakers until released at a time of ecstatic rapture.[65]

There is little question from a psychological perspective that this explanation is possible. There are too many clinical

---

[61]J. H. Michael, "The Gift of Tongues at Corinth," *The Expositor*, 4 (September 1907): 261, notes: "We come to the conclusion then that Paul refers to different languages or dialects *as an illustration* of the γλωσσολαλία. Would he do so if the γλωσσολαλία itself were foreign speech? A comparison implies a difference as well as a similarity. . . The very fact that Paul makes the comparison of verses 10 and 11 proves that speech in foreign languages was not part of the γλωσσολαλία at Corinth."

[62]Albert Moll, *Hypnotism* (Charles Scribner's Sons, 1913), p. 243.

[63]Morton Prince, *The Unconscious: The Fundamentals of Known Personality, Normal and Abnormal* (Macmillan and Company, 1913), p. 229.

[64]Arthur Wright, *Some New Testament Problems* (Methuen and Company, 1898), pp. 277-303.

[65]In connection with the Pentecost narrative Lindsay Dewar, *The Holy Spirit and Modern Thought* (A. R. Mombray and Company, 1959), p. 59, holds the diaspora Jews could have recognized "classical" Hebrew from their scriptures when it broke forth from the unconscious memories of those at Pentecost.

examples of an unlearned foreign language in the personal unconscious to deny a priori the existence of such phenomena.[66] There remains, however, for the biblical theologian, regardless of whether this is actually what happened at Corinth and Jerusalem, the task of determining *meaning*. It is difficult to understand Paul's position with respect to glossolalia, if in fact it were simply a foreign language. More difficult is it to account for its rather dramatic effect at Pentecost if it were only repressed foreign language. The clinical examples of this phenomenon today are not nearly so dramatic or impressive. Such a view undercuts the significance of glossolalia as a *charisma*, and voids the Pauline concept of the "gift of interpretation."[67]

Background of Glossolalia in Palestine

In view of the material in the Old Testament and in the inter-biblical sources, it seems relatively certain that the primary background for the Corinthian glossolalia was Hebraic and not Hellenistic; however, there was some modification of the phenomenon at Corinth. Philo, for example, enumerates four types of ecstasy: (1) mad fury producing mental delusion; (2) extreme amazement; (3) mental tranquility of vacancy; (4) divine possession or frenzy of the prophets.[68] He certainly has Plato's *Phaedras*[69] in mind since he employs the term μανία.[70] He described the ecstatic prophet as having "no utterance of his own, but all his utterances came from elsewhere, the echoes of another's voice. . . ."[71] Elsewhere Philo writes:

---

[66]For example see Shumway, op. cit., pp. 52ff. Cf. Cutten, op. cit., p. 176.

[67]Mosiman, op. cit., p. 33.

[68]Philo, *Who Is the Heir*, 249 in Ralph Marcus (trans.), *Philo*. "The Loeb Classical Library" (10 vols.; William Heinemann, 1939-1953), 5:409-11.

[69]See chapter 2.

[70]Philo, loc. cit., in Marcus, loc. cit.

[71]Philo, op. cit., 259 in Marcus, op. cit., p. 417.

> Nothing of what he says will be his own, for he that is truly
> under the control of divine inspiration has no power of ap-
> prehension when he speaks as the channel for the insistent
> words of another's prompting.[72]

Again, he states that divination is a corruption or a counterfeit
of the divine and prophetic possession.

> For no pronouncement of a prophet is even his own; he is an
> interpreter prompted by another in all utterances, when
> knowing not what he does he is filled with inspiration, as the
> reason withdraws and surrenders the citadel of the soul to a
> new visitor and tenant, the Divine spirit, which plays upon
> the vocal organism and dictates words which clearly express
> its prophetic message.[73]

It becomes clear, then, that Philo's concept of ecstatic prophecy was that of divine possession in which all conscious control by the prophet was abdicated to the Divine Spirit. While
there is no indication that these references describe a phenomenon parallel to the Corinthian glossolalia, it does furnish a
background which would tolerate such expressions of possession by the Spirit.

The closest that Philo comes to describing what was occurring at Corinth is when he describes the Hebrew name Han-
nah, which means "grace."

> When grace fills the soul, that soul thereby rejoices and
> smiles and dances, for it is possessed and inspired [βε-
> βαχχεύται], so that to many of the unenlightened it may
> seem to be drunken, crazy and beside itself. . . . For with the
> God-possessed [θεοφορήτοις] not only is the soul wont to be
> stirred and goaded as it were into ecstasy but the body also is
> flushed and fiery, warmed by the overflowing joy within
> which passes on the sensation to the outer man, and thus

---

[72]Philo, *On the Special Law Books*, I, 65 in Marcus, op. cit., 7:137.

[73]Philo, *On the Special Law Books*, IV, 49 in Marcus, op. cit., 8:37-
39.

many of the foolish are deceived and suppose that the sober are drunk.[74]

Maurice Barnett suggests the impossibility of a pagan cult having given rise to glossolalia at Corinth because Paul speaks of the attendant problems as though they were quite unfamiliar to the Corinthian Christians. In Barnett's view, this indicates that these Christians were in fact in need of instructions and guidance.[75] Following a suggestion made by T. W. Manson, Barnett theorizes that the Cephas party was seeking to impose upon the Christian community there the same type of ecstatic frenzy which had characterized the original outpouring of the Spirit at Pentecost. In keeping with their Judaistic ritual emphasis, the Cephas party was more interested in the external form than the essential meaning of the phenomenon. It was the requirement of this "party" that all Corinthian Christians who received the Spirit must show the same external signs indicating its presence.[76]

While it is not certain that the Cephas party was the Judaizing influence as Barnett claims, his point concerning the Corinthian problem being bound up with pagan excesses is relevant.

In every pagan rite or cult . . . the ecstatic experience was sought, and in many cases artificial means were used to induce a state of uncontrollable excitement, which became false ecstasy. But in the New Testament there is no artificiality; ecstasy comes first and the strange untterances are the outward

---

[74]Philo, *On Drunkenness*, 36, 146-47 in Marcus, op. cit., 3:395. H. A. Wolfson, *Philo* (2 vols.; Harvard University Press, 1947), 2:49-50, concludes that Philo is differentiating between the type of ecstasy which comes by the grace of God and that which is artifically induced by strong wine in the Bacchic frenzies of the followers of Dionysus.

[75]Barnett, op. cit., p. 106.

[76]Ibid., pp. 106-108.

sign of the inward condition. The spirit comes upon persons and then they speak with tongues.[77]

Quite possibly it was the artificiality with which Paul was dealing in the Corinthian letter. Perhaps the pagan practices in Corinth served only to confuse a stimulated ecstasy with the characteristic Hebraic "spirit possession" which came suddenly and unexpectedly upon a person. There may have been at Corinth the same problem of distinguishing between "ecstasy" and "true spirit possession" as existed in Israel when prophetism came into contact with the bands of Canaanite prophets.

Some scholars[78] have called attention to the fact that in isolated phrases and formulas Paul seems to indicate that at least the language of the pagan philosophies, e.g., Stoicism and Platonism, was current among the Corinthian Christians. On the other hand, certain scholars[79] note how Paul reinterpreted this terminology in the light of his own Hebrew background, his Rabbinic training, and his personal encounter with the Christ. It is, therefore, not proper to suggest that Paul's religion was a "syncretistic"[80] one; rather, the truth is that Paul was a rugged opponent of any syncretistic tendencies in the church at Corinth. Thus, it appears that Paul could not tolerate a type of ecstasy which isolated the individual from normal social relations with his fellow worshippers. As W. D. Davies notes:

---

[77]Ibid., p. 104.

[78]W. L. Knox, *St. Paul and the Church of the Gentiles* (Cambridge University Press, 1939), pp. 161ff.; C. H. Dodd, *The Bible and the Greeks* (Hodder and Stoughton, 1935), passim.

[79]W. D. Davies, *Paul and Rabbinic Judaism* (S. P. C. K., 1948), p. 180; W. D. Stacey, *The Pauline View of Man* (Macmillian and Company, 1956), p. 143; A. B. J. Rawlinson, *The New Testament Doctrine of the Christ* (Longmans, Green, and Company, 1926), p. 159.

[80]Quoted in H. A. A. Kennedy, *St. Paul and the Mystery-Religions* (Hodder and Stoughton, 1913), p. 30.

> Paul's conception of the Spirit in the light of Rabbinic Judaism
> . . . has one aspect which sets it wholly apart from what we
> found in Hellenism, mainly its communal character.[81]

Paul acknowledges the divine origin of glossolalia (1 Cor.
14:2), but he also reminds the Corinthians not to be excessive
in their practice of the gift (1 Cor. 14:27). Paul is seeking a
proper balance within the church life between the sensational
aspects of the Spirit and the more sedate and beneficial aspects of its endowment.

The issue is simply that the *charismata* were sometimes
made ends in themselves and eagerly sought for, not in a magical vein, but as signs of superiority over other Christians.
While certain individuals were eager for manifestations of the
presence of the Spirit, they did not use these manifestations to
build up the church (1 Cor. 14:12). Rather, those who excelled
in extraordinary gifts, particularly glossolalia, paraded them
(1 Cor. 13:4-5); they looked down upon less-gifted Christians
(1 Cor. 12:21); they often caused intolerable confusion in the
worship services (1 Cor. 14:33). Obviously, the seeking of *charismata* for their own sake led to the counterfeiting of them.[82]
Thus, the gift of distinguishing the true from the false manifestations became necessary. By the end of the New Testament
era, the problem had become acute:

> Beloved, do not believe every spirit, but test the spirits to see
> whether they are of God; for many false prophets have gone
> out into the world. By this you know the Spirit of God: every
> spirit which confesses that Jesus Christ has come in the flesh
> is of God, and every spirit which does not confess Jesus is not
> of God. By this we know the spirit of truth and the spirit of
> error (1 John 4:1-2, 4-6).

---

[81]Davies, op. cit., p. 200.

[82]At Corinth there were those who were so antithetical to the very
heart of the Christian *kerygma* that they could cry out "Jesus be
cursed" and claim to be speaking "by the Spirit of God." Cf. 1 Corinthians 12:3.

It is here suggested that the *charismata* and related phenomena are properly understood as a part of the Spirit witness to the *kerygma*. Hence the proper starting point is not 1 Corinthians 12-14, where there is a situation in which these *charismata* are being overemphasized, but rather, the passages where the *kerygma* is being preached and the Spirit bears witness to its validity. Thus approached, the *charismata* remain extraordinary and super-human, but not excessive or bizarre. They form a coherent picture, not of human auto-suggestion and mass excitement, but of the working of the Spirit whose power invades human life to bear witness to the truth of the *kerygma*.

Paul's main objection is not to the practice of glossolalia so much as to the *estimate* of the practice. In 1 Corinthians 12:1-3 he asserts that all Christians are πνευματικοί by virtue of their baptismal confession (1 Cor. 12:13). The entire twelfth chapter makes the basic point that there is diversity and equal authenticity among the various gifts of the Spirit. It appears that pneumatic status was being denied at Corinth to those who could not produce the more sensational signs like glossolalia, and claimed exclusively for those who did. That is to say, there is evidently the claim that tongues serve as a "sign" for the Christians.[83] It would be a simple step from tongues as "a" sign to tongues as "the" sign.

> The one and only reason which Paul gives for allowing the use of tongues in the presence of others is that they may serve to attract the attention of unbelievers, and even this seems to be curiously at variance with the later comment that "outsiders" coming in will think people who talk in tongues are mad—unless verse 22 refers to one single person talking in tongues and verse 23 to the confusion when several speak together.[84]

---

[83]It is unlikely that the sign-value of tongues is an original contribution of Paul's; his other references to signs are few and mostly critical. Cf. 2 Thessalonians 2:9; 2 Corinthians 12:12; 1 Corinthians 1:22.

[84]"Notes on Recent Exposition," *Expository Times*, 78 (May 1966): 227.

It is important, then, to distinguish glossolalia from the *problem* of glossolalia. As J. P. M. Sweet concludes: "The problem, . . . was new, and lay not in a surfeit of, but in a demand for, glossolalia. . . ."[85] If Paul were not attacking tongues per se, but rather the estimate of their value, then his positive statements can be allowed to speak for themselves. Evidence outside the epistle itself indicates that Paul's attitude was reserved but not altogether negative: Paul recognizes tongues as a *charisma*, but his concept of *charisma* is substantially different from that of the Corinthians. To them the *charisma* was something extraordinary and supernatural. To Paul, however, it was something more. Specifically, the *charisma*, is the expression of the church's διαχονία.[86] Thus, for the service of others, νοῦς is essential.[87]

In light of the foregoing discussion, what conclusions may be drawn from the Corinthians pericope concerning glossolalia? The following are suggested: (1) Paul rejects the claim that tongues are the exclusive (1 Cor. 12:30) or even the normal sign of the presence of the Spirit of God. (2) His condemnation of glossolalia is not absolute, but in relation to other *charisma* (1 Cor. 16:6-10, 12:28-30). While he valued it highly as a private experience (1 Cor. 14:4; cf. 1 Cor. 14:18-19). Since it was private it could not effect οἰχοδομή, and therefore he regarded it inferior to those activities that could (1 Cor. 14:8). (3) Paul does not regard glossolalia as childish; but rather it is the Corinthians' estimate of it that he considers childish. He was anxious that the Corinthian Christians should not allow their idea of the spiritual to be narrowed to a point where it would be dom-

---

[85]Sweet, op. cit., p. 249.

[86]Cf. 1 Corinthians 12. See H. J. Schoeps, *Paul*, trans. Harold Knight (Lutterworth Press, 1961), pp. 68-69.

[87]C. E. B. Cranfield, *A Commentary on Romans 12-13* (Oliver and Boyd, 1965), p. 14, argues that λογιχὴν λατρεία means not *spiritual* as opposed to *external*, but rational as opposed to irrational, or ecstatic.

inated by the least valuable gift (1 Cor. 12:6-10, 12:28-30, 14:3). (4) It is all but impossible to claim Pauline authority for regarding glossolalia as a necessary part of the Christian life in light of the conspicuous absence of any reference to tongues in Romans 12, as compared to 1 Corinthians 12. On the other hand, it is obviously fallacious to claim that Paul held them to be devil-inspired and completely without value.

Paul's ambivalence, then, can be explained partially by the danger of allowing tongues to become the sole "sign" of the presence of God's Spirit. There may well have been an additional reason for his apparent ambivalence in connection with the spiritual value of this gift. Perhaps the relationship of Acts to 1 Corinthians with respect to glossolalia is indicative of this point. To this important consideration the discussion now turns.

THE RELATIONSHIP OF ACTS AND 1 CORINTHIANS

Earlier it was suggested that Luke added the foreign language motif to the account in Acts 2. There are several possible motivations, and Luke's redaction may have been the result of any one or combination of these factors.

Jewish Parallels

The theophany at Mount Sinai. Some scholars note that Luke seems to have had in the background of his thought the giving of the law at Sinai. Could it be that Luke describes the phenomenon the way he does, not because he misunderstood glossolalia, but because he wanted to emphasize the parallels to the theophany at Sinai?[88] There can be little doubt that the giving of the law is in the background of Luke's thought. The wind, the tongues of fire and even the glossolalia itself, all resemble the manifestations of the Spirit of God at Sinai. Fur-

---

[88]Elmer H. Zaugg, *A Genetic Study of the Spirit Phenomena in the New Testament* (University of Chicago Press, 1917), passim. See further Hermann L. Strack and Paul Billerbeck, *Kommentar zum Neuen Testament und Talmud und Midrasch* (6 vols.; Beck, 1922-1961), 2:604ff.

thermore, the contrast of the age of the law and the new age of the Spirit is self-evident. The Jews taught that the law was given so that it was understood in all languages:

> Although the ten commandments were promulgated with a single sound it says, "all people heard the voices"; it follows then that when the voice went forth it was divided into seven voices, and then went into seventy tongues, and every people received the law in their own language.[89]

The Tower of Babel. Another Old Testament parallel which has fascinated scholars is the story of the Tower of Babel. The obvious contrast between the Babel story and the Pentecostal experience may well have been in Luke's mind when he wrote his narrative. According to Philo, in the beginning man had only one language which was intelligible to all humans.[90] The confusion of men's languages occurred at the building of the Tower of Babel. Evidently, there was the expectation that at some time in the future the people of the Lord would again have one language.[91] Apparently there was a disagreement as to what the language would be, i.e., Hebrew, Syriac, Greek, or Aramaic.[92]

J. G. Davies[93] made a significant contribution in this area when he compared the Greek of the Pentecost narrative with

---

[89]Midrash Tahuma quoted in Dale Moody, *Spirit of the Living God* (Westminster Press, 1968), p. 72.

[90]Philo, *The Confusion of Tongues*, III, 6 in Marcus, op. cit., 4:13. Cf. Josephus, *Jewish Antiquities*, I, 40, 4 in H. St. J. Thackeray (trans.), *Josephus*. "The Loeb Classical Library" (8 vols.; William Heinemann, 1930-1938), 4:21.

[91]*Testament of the XII Patriarchs*, Judah 25:3 in R. H. Charles, *The Apocrypha and Pseudophigrapha of the Old Testament in English* (2 vols.; Clarendon Press, 1913), 2:324.

[92]Charles, op. cit., II, 17.

[93]J. G. Davies, "Pentecost and Glossolalia," *Journal of Theological Studies*, 3 (1952): 228-31.

that of the Septuagint account of the Tower Babel. Genesis 11:7 reads, in the LXX, "Go to, let us down and there confound [συγχεῶμεν] their language [γλῶσσα], that they may not understand [ἀκούσωσιν] one another's speech [φωνῆς]." On the day of Pentecost the Disciples "were filled with the Holy Spirit and began to speak in other tongues [λῶσσαις], as the Spirit gave them utterance." Luke continues: "And at this sound [φωνῆς] the multitude came together and they were bewildered [συνεχύθη]."

This linguistic comparison indicates Luke's dependence upon the Genesis story for some of his *vocabulary* used to express the experience; however, little more can be safely claimed.

Pauline Influence

Another theory which might account for Luke's shaping of the primitive account so as to include the foreign language motif is tied to Luke's relationship with Paul. It is suggested that Luke, under Pauline influence, sought to reinterpret the original speaking in tongues so as to avoid the Pauline criticism concerning disorder and unintelligibility. The position regarding the dating of Luke and 1 Corinthians adopted here would allow his theory. Also, the theory that Luke and Paul were in fact traveling companions has given credence to this position. Furthermore, to carry the argument an additional step, the acquaintance of Luke and Paul could explain not only the alteration in the Lukan narrative, but also, in some measure, account for Paul's ambivalence on the subject of glossolalia. If Luke did avail himself of sources, however, disputed and undefined, it is reasonable to assume that the Corinthian Christians heard of this Jerusalem "tradition." Paul's respect for Luke, as well as the close association of the events of Pentecost with the apostles, among which he sought diligently to be numbered himself, could in some small way help explain his refusal to condemn the phenomenon per se, despite the serious reservations which he had when he learned of the excesses at Corinth.

Psychological Communication

Again, Luke may have taken the view that the communication which transpired at Pentecost was not a type of speech which would be intelligible to a disinterested spectator; however, within the context of the community it was nevertheless a form of language which, under the right conditions and by the proper people, could be understood; but language itself is not always necessary for communication and understanding.[94] He points out that there was a "subsoil" of devoutness among those who "heard." The Holy Spirit energized this kind of communication among those who were a part of this community. Oates concludes that this type of communication is

> highly communal—those who understand each other eat together in gladness and singleness of heart. This understanding is reciprocal—no one person is left to do all the understanding in one-way communication.[95]

While this "type" of community might well have been reflected in the Pentecost narrative, it is most unlikely what it existed in even the remotest form at Corinth. In fact, 1 Corinthians would seem to indicate that it did not.

From the questions to which Paul addressed himself in that epistle it appears that the Corinthian church was problem-ridden. There was division among the membership there. (1 Cor. 1:10ff.). A certain individual was evidently living with his father's wife, and the church apparently was indifferent to the situation (1 Cor. 5:1-13). Church members were suing one another in pagan courts of law (1 Cor. 6:1-11). Some of the Christians were turning grace into license, and Paul had to remind them that members of the body of Christ must not give their own bodies to harlots (1 Cor. 6:15). Others boasted over

---

[94]Wayne E. Oates, "The Holy Spirit and the Overseer of the Flock," *Review and Expositor*, 63 (Spring 1966): 188.

[95]Ibid.

their knowledge (1 Cor. 8), while still others selfishly employed freedom to the hurt of others in the name of personal "rights" (1 Cor. 9). The services of worship were disorderly (1 Cor. 11:1-6), and some turned the Lord's Supper into a private supper club with clannish indulgences (1 Cor. 11:17-34). Certainly Corinth, then, was lacking as a community where psychological communication might take place.

Any or all of these reasons might account for Luke's particular slant in his presentation of the material in the Pentecost narrative. The main contention is that 1 Corinthians deals with a particular historical situation where the concept of the Spirit of God as power is absent. The result is division and disunity.

CONCLUSION

The following statements are offered as a concluding summary of this chapter of the dissertation.

(1) Tongues are obviously alluded to, and specifically mentioned in 1 Corinthians.

(2) Paul is ambivalent in his attitude, i.e., he confesses that he speaks with tongues "more than you all," yet he calls for certain restrictions in the practice of glossolalia among the Corinthian Christians. The former position is the natural outgrowth of his (a) association with Luke; (b) knowledge of the Pentecost tradition; (c) desire to demonstrate his apostleship. The latter position stems from his observations which indicate to him the vast difference between Corinthian and Pentecostal glossolalia. He realizes that (a) in the light of the Greek ecstatic background Corinthian glossolalia may be only an imitation of the Pentecostal concept of possession by the Spirit; (b) there is an excessive demand for glossolalia to the *the* sign of spirit possession; (c) that there ought to be order in worship and church life; (d) all spiritual gifts ought to build up the church and issue forth in service.

(3) Finally, Paul's *basic* theory of the validity of tongues is not at variance with Luke's. The difference lies rather in the significance being attached to the phenomenon. In keeping

with the concept of the Spirit of God which manifests itself through the several gifts of the Spirit, and in light of the particular historical setting in which the church at Corinth found itself, it appears that to interpret glossolalia theologically for the church today, one ought to consider the Lukan material on the subject as primary.

5

A THEOLOGICAL INTERPRETATION OF GLOSSOLALIA

The real incentive for studying glossolalia grows out of the conviction that—despite the legitimacy of its conclusions—its existence today points to the fact that there is a less than adequate theology of the Spirit extant in the church presently. Indeed, for most observers, the issue is not speaking in tongues, per se; rather, it is what this phenomenon says (or does not say) about the nature of the Spirit that is ultimately important.

On one level, much of the disagreement concerning glossolalia today would subside or disappear altogether, if there could be a distinction drawn between the structural (formal) and the symbolic meanings of the phenomenon. Some noncharismatic scholars who reject "speaking in tongues" a priori because of its objective offensiveness would not hesitate to envision some other role for the Holy Spirit in the lives of contemporary Christians. Similarly, by focusing upon the totality of the phenomena that may attest to the Spirit's presence, and by viewing glossolalia as one of these, some glossolalists might refrain from regarding their gift as superior to all others. Some contemporary Christians will inevitably "stumble" at the *form* of glossolalia; but these same Christians might accept the notion that this structure *once* represented the power and presence of God in the early church. Thus while not accepting the form, they might well share a similar belief about the availability of God's power and presence in the world today.

In other words, when glossolalia first appeared in Christian circles, persons of other religious persuasions commonly accepted the practice as a mark of possession by the gods. It undoubtedly made a profound impression on these people and a strong witness for the faith. But the world view today is so much different that some people look upon tongue speaking as a sign of insanity or even fanaticism—a displaced sign of an age long past.

The question is "what value is there in a demythologized glossolalia?" Perhaps a point of departure for discovering that value, if any, may emerge if a distinction is drawn between the formal structure and symbolic meaning of glossolalia.

THE FORMAL STRUCTURE OF GLOSSOLALIA

The Reality of Glossolalia

That the experience that we now refer to as glossolalia occurred among the earlier Christians cannot be denied. Further, instances of similar phenomena can be documented outside Christendom, as well as in the history of the Christian church. While occurring in the first century, there is now reason to assume that glossolalia was unique to that age.[1] The

---

[1]Some scholars dismiss glossolalia as a phenomenon which occurred *only* in the first century, thus being, in reality, a temporary gift of the apostolic church. Cf. Anthony A. Hoekema, *What About Tongue-Speaking?* (Eerdmans, 1966), pp. 103-13; Zane C. Hodges, "The Purpose of Tongues," *Bibliotheca Sacra*, 120 (1963): 226-33. Imposing such a rigid dichotomy upon history, of course, has serious theological consequences.

problem arises in identifying the *precise* nature of the *formal* structure of glossolalia, particularly in Acts. The ambiguous phrase ἑτέραις γλώσσαισ in Acts 2:4 leaves the question open of whether we should understand glossolalia or foreign tongues. If the latter is intended, then why the reference to the accompanying ecstatic state in verses 7 and 12? Of the former, why the list of the peoples present (Acts 1:5, 9-11). Perhaps Luke has interpreted the tradition of an event of charismatic religion, specifically ecstatic speech, *away* from the kind of thing which no one really understood and in favor of an intelligible foreign language motif. This "interpretation" would extend his theme of the universality of the Gospel.

If such an interpretation is correct, what conclusions may be stated, on the basis of the present inquiry concerning the formal nature of glossolalia.

Definition. Glossolalia is the spontaneous utterance of uncomprehended and seemingly random vocal sounds. These sounds often have a rhythm best perhaps akin to Calypso music. A transliterated example is:

> Prou pray praddy
> Pa palassate pa pau pu pe
> Heli terratte taw
> Terrei te te-te-te
> Vole virte vum
> Elee lete leele luto
> Sine sirge singe
> Imba imba imba

While the speech itself often appears effortless, with repetitions and inflections characteristic of a language, linguists consistently maintain that objectively the samples examined correspond to no language known to mankind. This conclusion is reached in spite of hundreds, if not thousands, of *testimonia*. Of course, not one of these has been recorded and subsequently verified by linguists. Communication, if present at all, transpires on the psychological level and thus is not contingent upon the identification of the glossolalia with some specific language of mankind.

Origin. Glossolalia probably evolved out of the desire of religious converts and devotees to have some specific, "objective" proof of their being possessed by the Spirit of God. Objectively, a spectator would witness an overpowering demonstration of frenzied, inarticulate, incoherent, ecstatic speech when the glossolalist became "filled with the Spirit." The prominence afforded glossolalia is easily understood when we recall its striking, sensational, and appealing character. In fact, these attributes are so evident an indication of its unusual power, the deity alone could give it. For this reason, the experience became a standard, par-excellence, for indicating one's favor with the divine.[2]

Effects. There is evidence that glossolalia gave the impression of being incoherent, maudlin talk issuing forth from persons who were inebriated. It appears that neither the Pentecostal event itself nor any of the subsequent manifestations of the Spirit's presence has had any significant apologetic thrust among the non-participants. Luke tells us that some of the crowd scoffed at this manifestation of the Spirit, linking it with the "babbling" of drunkards. Luke represents Peter as the one who shrewdly proceeds to defend the actions of the disciples who uttered these strange sounds. Peter spoke in his ordinary tongue; however, communication was effective, judging from the results of his preaching (Acts 2:41).

At Corinth the *charismata* were made ends in themselves and sought after as signs of superiority to be used superciliously over other Christians. The Christians there were "eager for manifestations of the Spirit," but apparently they did not use them to build up the church (1 Cor. 14:12). Those who excelled in extraordinary gifts, particularly glossolalia, paraded them (1 Cor. 13:4-5); they looked down upon the less-gifted Christians (1 Cor. 12:21); and they produced intolerable confusion in the services of worship (1 Cor. 14:33). In time,

---

[2]Ira J. Martin, "The Place and Significance of Glossolalia in the New Testament" (unpublished doctor's dissertation, Boston University, 1942), p. 108.

those who sought the various *charismata* for their own sake began to counterfeit these gifts. Thus, the gift of distinguishing the true from the false became necessary. At the close of the first century the problem had become acute:

> Beloved, do not believe every spirit, but test the spirits to see whether they are of God; for many false prophets have gone out into the world. By this you know the Spirit of God: every spirit which confesses that Jesus Christ has come in the flesh is of God (1 John 4:1-2).

Thus, the writer of 1 John indicates that the Christian could no longer trust what appeared to be the "working" of the Spirit. Rather, he must carefully examine "every spirit."

Value. While Paul saw no value in glossolalia for the church as a whole (1 Cor. 14:2, 14:4, 14:5, 14:19, 14:28), he evidently recognized some personal reward for the individual who spoke in tongues. Also, Paul realized that glossolalia might serve as a "sign" that could convince an unbeliever that God existed and exerted his power upon people.[3] Perhaps Paul best expresses his estimate of glossolalia when he wrote:

> . . . in church I would rather speak five words with my mind, in order to instruct others, than ten thousand words in a tongue (1 Cor. 14:19).

Thus, while Paul did not deny that glossolalia was a valid *charisma*, he did deny that it was to be exalted to first place as *the* sole evidence of the indwelling of God's Spirit. In fact, the apostle noted that it was inferior to prophecy (1 Cor. 14:5), and in his listings, tongue speech was last (1 Cor. 12:10). Yet Paul was unwilling to write off the phenomenon completely, indicating that it could be a meaningful part of the worship service provided certain regulations were adhered to: (1) there should

---

[3]Cf. J. P. M. Sweet, "A Sign for Unbelievers: Paul's Attitude to Glossolalia," *New Testament Studies*, 13 (April 1967): 24-267. Cf. James Alston Marrow, "The Holy Spirit in the Book of Acts" (unpublished master's thesis, Union Theological Seminary 1952), p. 115.

not be more than three glossolalists speaking during a single service (1 Cor. 14:27); (2) of those allowed to speak, only one should speak at a time (1 Cor. 14:27); (3) and this one should speak only when an interpreter is present (1 Cor. 14:27); (4) without an interpreter, and if the glossolalist could not interpret, the gift has no legitimate place in public worship services (1 Cor. 14:25).

Luke, on the other hand, does not assess the value of the gift, per se; however, his writings presuppose belief in a God whose Spirit is active in the proclamation of the gospel—a God who vindicates the work of the apostles by demonstrating through some sign his presence and power.

Dangers. According to Paul's own teaching (Gal. 5:16-26) the indwelling of the Spirit was a legitimate requisite to the Christian life, as was the demonstration of this indwelling; however, because glossolalia had become the standard whereby all charismatic gifts were to be judged, Paul advocated strict controls in connection with its use. Glossolalia tested the presence of the Spirit by external signs, which of themselves had no inherent value. On the contrary, at Corinth these "signs" had degenerated into the sensational, the showy, the gaudy. The Corinthian Christians appeared to have overlooked the fact that the demonstration of the Spirit's presence ought to reflect to some degree the character of that spirit itself. Paul emphasized this when he developed love as the greatest of all the *charismata* (1 Cor. 13:13), and the evidence of this quality "most excellent" is drawn from the indwelling of the Spirit of God.

> But the fruit of the Spirit is love, joy, peace, patience, kindness, goodness, faithfulness, gentleness, self-control . . . (Gal. 5:22-23a. Cf. Eph. 5:9).

It is in this dangerous, subversive, misleading interpretation of glossolalia as *the* standard of the indwelling of the Spirit—consciously or unconsciously implied—that Paul saw the real menace of glossolalia.

A Critical Evaluation of the Formal Structure of Glossolalia

It is understandable why the Christians of the first century elected to let glossolalia signify the belief that the Holy Spirit had come upon them. The early church was born and grew in a hostile environment, and an outward visible sign of the Spirit's presence was necessary to indicate to the unbelievers that the work of the gospel was legitimate. Accepted as a valid sign of the Spirit's presence by those early Christians, speaking in tongues gave external objectification to the conviction that God's power was indwelling in the individual.

Today, for the mainstream of Protestantism, public instances of glossolalia bring confusion, disunity and disillusionment. From the perspective of many non-glossolalists, speaking in tongues is a weird, esoteric phenomenon that belongs to immature Christians of a low socio-economic background who possess a fundamentalist understanding of life and the faith. But these "mainstream" Christians are viewed by glossolalists as lacking the "baptism of the Spirit" and the deep commitment to the faith that this expression signals. Their Christian witness is conspicuously marked by the absence of this "second blessing" that comes when the Christian receives the baptism of the Spirit. While the non-glossolalists point to the whole context of glossolalia as a "highly charged atmosphere," the glossolalists note that the phenomenon "can also occur in quiet surroundings, and the unleashing of emotionalism is simply not a necessary part of speaking in tongues."[4] While some critics of the tongues movement dismiss it as "praying in gibberish,"[5] its defenders point to the results of the study done by Morton T. Kelsey, a disciple of Jung:

It seems to be a physical impossibility to duplicate tongue-

---

[4]Morton T. Kelsey, *Tongue Speaking: An Experiment in Spiritual Experience* (Doubleday & Company 1964), p. 1.

[5]"Taming the Tongues," *Time*, 84 (July 10, 1964): 66. Cf. Stuart Bergsma, *Speaking in Tongues* (Baker Book House 1965), p. 24.

speech by deliberate imitation; when gibberish is produced
by conscious effort, this also produces muscular tension
which soon differentiates the sounds from the effortless flow
of glossolalia.[6]

These observations point to the mounting difficulties that separate those pro and con. Certainly, both the defenders of glossolalia and the remainder of Christendom must share the
burden of compromise if these difficulties are to be overcome.

A reconstructed non-glossolalist position. The apostle Paul
wrote:

> So, my brethren, earnestly desire to prophesy, and do not for-
> bid speaking in tongues; but all things should be done de-
> cently and in order (1 Cor. 14:39-40).

Here, Paul does advocate certain legislative controls for the exercise of glossolalia; but he does not forbid the phenomenon
among the Corinthian Christians. Paul does, however, rec-
ommend that the Christians at Corinth seek a more important
gift—prophesying (1 Cor. 14:39). Here, Paul probably meant
the intelligent expression of the reality and power of God and
of his redemptive work and purposes among men. Even
though Paul ranks glossolalia low in terms of the relative value
of spiritual gifts, he nonetheless *gives it status as a gift.* The task
of the non-glossolalist Christian is two-fold: (1) recognize glossolalia as a legitimate, non-normative experience that may attest to the presence of God's Spirit in the life of those who
practice it; (2) recognize that important lessons and insights
can be learned from charismatic Christians. The structure of
glossolalia may be pointing up the sometimes cold, imper-
sonal form that institutional worship has acquired.[7] Glossolalia may point up a sterile, over-intellectualized and over-
organized Christianity.

---

[6]Kelsey, op. cit., p. 6.

[7]John P. Newport, "Speaking with Tongues," *Home Missions*, 36
(May 1965): 22.

Glossolalists have demonstrated a genuine zeal and commitment to the Christian faith that is matched by few traditional denominations. This may be so because the charismatics have set definite spiritual goals that are to be achieved, and because they have well developed methods to achieve them. Regardless of how non-participants view the objective manifestation of glossolalia, only the most narrow-minded Christian would proceed to "write off" charismatic religion as totally insignificant and irrelevant.

A reconstructed glossolalist position. The glossolalist must also lend a sympathetic ear to those who are skeptical of the worth of random speech sounds as a valid symbol for the presence of God's Spirit. The serious glossolalist who is concerned about meaningful dialog with the non-glossolalist might consider the following: (1) recognize that while glossolalia is *a* legitimate symbol it is not the *sole* symbol that expresses the presence of God's Spirit, and consequently it is not normative for all Christians. A non-glossolalist who rejects the experience as an acceptable indication of the presence of the Spirit, may at the same time be searching elsewhere for a more relevant symbol. The charismatic must not view as a threat the estimate of glossolalia that relegates it to the place of

> a completely irrational symbol which demands total surrender of one's inhibitions, intellectual capacities, pride or anything else which stands in the way of one's total surrender to God.[8]

One individual who spoke in tongues described the experience this way:

> I heard of a group of people . . . who had had a dynamic experience of the Spirit and manifested the gifts of tongues. I was filled with question being a rather conservative person, and of a rather intellectual bent, but I was more filled with an awareness that these people really had something vital in

---

[8]Lester D. Cleveland, "Let's Demythologize Glossolalia," *The Baptist Program*, 45 (June 1967): 11.

their Christian living that I needed and wanted. So I took the leap and joined their group . . . earnestly seeking the Holy Spirit and whatever gifts he might want to give me. [The] willingness to receive the gift of tongues was a real turning point, because that willingness—to be a fool for Christ—involved a new degree of surrender, which made it possible for the Spirit to come. Needless to say, he did come in great overwhelming power and joy. . . . [9]

In this case history, as in many others, the symbol is relatively *unimportant*, while the total surrender is *absolutely necessary and all important*.[10] The tongue speaker should allow his non-glossolalist brother a degree of freedom in choosing other symbols that may be as meaningful as glossolalia is for the charismatics. What other gifts are there that might symbolize the Spirit's presence in the life of a non-glossolalist?

Again, inspect the theology of the Apostle Paul. For him, everyone has the Spirit, all have become spiritual so that, without exception, everyone is given a ministry. For Paul there can be neither a Christian nor a spiritual life without the presence of the Spirit. The diversity of ministries comes exclusively from and through the Spirit who gives to each person *what he will* (1 Cor. 12:11). It is a fundamental tenet of Paul's theology that the unity of the Spirit is concretely seen in the varieties of spiritual gifts. Everybody receives a gift, Paul says, but there are different ones (Rom. 12:3ff; 1 Cor. 12:4ff). In fact, life in the Christian community is always the inter-play of the various members who possess different spiritual gifts. The unity of the Spirit is not in the sameness of the specific gifts, but rather

---

[9]Quoted in Fred B. Morris, "Now I Want You All to Speak in Tongues . . .," *The Christian Advocate*, 7 (July 4, 1963): 9-10.

[10]The term "surrender" is a familiar one to the psychiatrist. The Christian may speak of surrender to the Spirit of God, while a psychiatrist refers to the surrender of the rational and conscious to the "irrational" or "transitional" and unconscious. Thus, the action of surrender may bring, psychologically speaking, a true sense of release and freedom.

in the fact that *all* the diverse gifts come from the same source. (2) Avoid the kind of statement that concludes that glossolalia is clearly superior to all other gifts.[11] Regardless of how one feels about glossolalia the words of Paul are clear:

> Now there are varieties of gifts, but the same Spirit; and there are varieties of service, but the same Lord; and there are varieties of workings, but it is the same God who inspires them all in every one. To each is given the manifestation of the Spirit for the common good. To one is given through the Spirit the utterance of wisdom, and to another the utterance of knowledge according to the same Spirit, to another faith by the same Spirit, to another gifts of healing by the one Spirit, to another the working of miracles, to another prophecy, to another the ability to distinguish between spirit, to another various kinds of tongues, to another the interpretation of tongues (1 Cor. 12:4-10).

Larry Christenson, a leader or the charismatic movement, recognizes that the experience of glossolalia is only *one* gift of the Spirit.[12] He claims the glossolalist does not pray for the gift of tongues, but rather for the gift of the Holy Spirit. Those who have not received this specific gift, therefore, should not be regarded as inferior by the glossolalists, nor should the former reject the latter because they have found meaning in tongue speech.[13] His central conclusion for the church today is that glossolalia is a valuable experience—one that should not be forbidden. He asks Christian love and understanding from those who have not had this experience as well as from those who have, as each seeks to relate to the other. (3) Realize that a rejection of glossolalia by a non-glossolalist does not consti-

---

[11]Cf. John Sherrill, *They Speak with Other Tongues* (Revell, 1964), p. 19, and *Methodists and the Baptism of the Holy Spirit* (Full Gospel Business Men's Fellowship International, 1963), p. 22.

[12]Quoted in Kelsey, op. cit., pp. 126ff.

[13] Tod W. Ewald, "Aspects of Tongues," *The Living Church*, 146 (June 2, 1963): 13.

tute a rejection of the place of the Holy Spirit in the Christian life. Many non-glossolalists know that the Holy Spirit is active and powerful; however, they expect the Spirit to manifest itself not in spectacular demonstrations but rather in the Christian graces mentioned in Galatians:

> . . . the fruit of the Spirit is love, joy, peace, patience, kindness, goodness, faithfulness, gentleness, self-control (Gal. 5:22-23a).

Conclusion. Both glossolalists and non-glossolalists alike must exercise spiritual maturity as they seek to examine the other's estimate of the external form of glossolalia. Each group has its differing estimates of the significance of this outward manifestation of the Spirit's presence.

THE MEANING OF GLOSSOLALIA

H. B. Swete noted in 1919 that:

> the spiritual element in the primitive γλωσσολαλία lay not in the strange utterances themselves, but in the elevation of heart and mind by which men were enabled to "magnify God."[14]

In terms of its objective form, glossolalia cannot be said to be a religious phenomenon per se, since phenomena identical in sound and psychological effect can occur in a non-religious context; therefore, the inherent meaning of the phenomenon must transcend its formal structure.

The Meaning of Biblical Glossolalia

Taken at face value, the Pentecost event made a tremendous impression upon all those present. Even if Luke redacted the tradition, other texts in Acts appear to undercover the centrality of the Pentecostal experience (Acts 4:31, 10:44-48, 19:2-7).

---

[14]H. B. Swete, *The Holy Spirit in the New Testament* (Macmillan and Company, 1919), p. 382.

At Pentecost, a soul-stirring experience dynamically affected the lives of those converts who were sensitized to and expectant of some great revelation from God. Consequently a number of those present broke forth spontaneously into ecstatic, involuntary speech. Without hesitation Luke has Peter attributing this demonstration to the action of the Holy Spirit (Acts 2:33, 2:28). Glossolalia was accepted as evidence of possession by the Spirit of God. For the converts it was a manifestation of the inflowing of the divine Spirit—the Spirit of power. While the phenomenon was not mechanical or induced, a significant religious realization lay behind it.

Great religious movements are usually accompanied by strong emotion which affects whole groups of people. Glossolalia under religious auspices is an emotional experience, but the presence of emotion alone neither accredits nor discredits the experience.[15]

This experience was evidently so impressive that others, encouraged by Peter's promise of a share in such an experience, began to seek it so that they might share in the power that lay behind it.

Luke intended his readers to understand that the converts of the Jesus-faith received the Spirit, and that this Spirit came in *power*. This indwelling of God's Spirit became the *sine qua non* of their teaching and practice (Acts 2:38). For Paul it may even have become an essential requirement—a standard for conversion and religious experience of all the followers of Jesus. His letters indicate that converts must not only have the spirit, but they must also *demonstrate* their possession of it (cf. Gal. 5:16, 5:22, 5:22). He maintained that the Spirit was supposed to reveal its presence in the believers by special means, i.e., the development of particular powers, gifts and graces that could only be accounted for by the presence of God's Spirit of power. Paul offers specific instances of these χαρίσ-

---

[15]Quoted in Charles William Shumway, "A Critical History of Glossolalia" (unpublished doctor's dissertation, Boston University, 1919), p. 67.

ματα (1 Cor. 12:10, 12:28-31).[16] Among these "gifts" is that of glossolalia.

Seen in this context—*a* gift of the Spirit—what did the glossolalia in Acts signify? One evident feature of the phenomenon is that the vocal sounds were addressed to God. This point should not be neglected as it is indicative of the *meaning* of glossolalia. Luke indicates that they heard them speaking in tongues and extolling God (Acts 10:46a). Paul points out to the Corinthians that "one who speaks in a tongue speaks not to men but to God (1 Cor. 14:2a). Probably glossolalia was not intended to convey a message to men; rather, it was a form of prayer (1 Cor. 14:14, 14:16). It was an effort to express to God the inexpressible: the indwelling of the Spirit of God. When the truth of the kerygma sank home to a responsive heart, ordinary human language was too restrictive to express the depth of the emotions that were aroused; therefore, one reaction was to break into ecstatic speech. This speech became an objective witness to the reality of the *kerygma*. The *charismata*, then, are to be understood as a part of the Spirit's witness to the *kerygma*.

> Approached in this fashion, the *charismata* remain extraordinary and super-human, but they are no longer bizarre and excessive. They make up a coherent picture, not of human autosuggestion and mass excitement, but of the working of a Spirit whose power invades human life to witness to the truth of the Gospel.[17]

A Critical Evaluation of the Meaning of Glossolalia

(1) All Christians need to recognize that there is a place for the Spirit of God in the church today. The various Pentecostal

---

[16]Χάρισμα is a little used word of late origin. It occurs in the New Testament only in the Pauline writings (except for a single instance in 1 Pet. 4:10).

[17]Albert Curry Winn, "*Pneuma* and *Kerygma*: a New Approach to the New Testament Doctrine of the Holy Spirit" (unpublished doctor's dissertation, Union Theological Seminary, 1956), p. 74.

sects and others who manifest glossolalia have chosen not to suppress "speech about God." They are seeking, however misguided from the non-glossolalist's view, to give meaning and content to their belief that God's Spirit moves spontaneously in the church and in individual lives.

One enduring contribution of charismatic religion is that it has forced the more "respectable" denominations to take a hard look at the doctrine of the Holy Spirit. Wayne Oates feels that religion is the "delicate" subject of this generation, and there is a certain shyness and inarticulateness when it comes to "talking" about God.[18] For this reason—and others—he defends the glossolalist:

> The persons who speaks [sic] in tongues cannot be 'written off' as a fanatic, a sick person, or a fool. We do not know how to pray as we ought. Therefore, these tongue speakings may be the 'sighs too deep for words.' On the other hand, they may become extremely meaningful to us personally whether they mean anything else to anyone else or not.[19]

In general there is a feeling among many Christians that charismatic behavior is not genuine. Rudolph Otto's charge is relevant:

> That . . . [the] church has lost its 'charisma,' that men look back to it as a thing of past times, that men make it and the inbreaking kingdom belonging to it trivial by allegories, does not show that . . . [the] church is now on a higher level, but is a sign of the decay.[20]

Into this "spiritual vacuum" the glossolalists bring a needed

---

[18]Wayne E. Oates, "A Socio-Psychological Study of Glossolalia," in Frank Stagg, E. Glenn Hinson and Wayne E. Oates, *Glossolalia: Tongue Speaking in Biblical, Historical, and Psychological Perspective* (Abingdon Press, 1967): 79.

[19]Ibid., p. 77.

[20]Rudolph Otto, *The Kingdom of God and the Son of Man* (Lutterworth Press, 1938), p. 376.

emphasis upon the role of the Holy Spirit. If it does not afford the individual and the community meaningful channels through which to express conviction that God's Spirit is working, the organized, institutional church will be ultimately irrelevant to the needs of mankind. Bishop Pike is correct in his analysis:

> Proponents of this [glossolalist] movement are indubitably right that our Church is in need of a greater sense of the activity of the Holy Spirit in the here and now and a greater resultant zeal of the Mission of the Church, for a change in lives and for personal testimony to Christ.[21]

(2) The glossolalist groups need to be more creative in developing and articulating a theology of glossolalia, i.e., what the phenomenon means for the Christian life. A telling weakness of the majority of glossolalist literature is the conspicuous absence of statements indicating what specific *relevance* glossolalia has for the Christian life. Rather frequently one gets the impression that the *experience* per se is what is being sought. *Eternity* magazine describes how a group will gather about a seeker and lay hands on his head. The seeker will be urged to use some foreign words he knows to start the flow. In addition he might be advised to let his jaw become loose and his tongue limp. Or he might be asked to repeat the name of Jesus over and over with great rapidity until he begins to stammer. "Now you are getting it," the group will tell the seeker.[22]

It would appear that within the ranks of some glossolalists there is the presupposition that a spiritual blessing *must* be attested to by means of a physical phenomenon. This is a difficult position to defend especially when some prominent Pentecostal writers concede that the tongue speaking that oc-

---

[21]James A. Pike, "Pastoral Letter Regarding 'Speaking in Tongues,'" *Pastoral Psychology*, 15 (May 1964): 57.

[22]Quoted in Newport, op. cit., p. 23.

curred at Corinth had nothing directly to do with being filled with the Spirit.[23] Paul took a different stance in Galatians:

> But the fruit of the Spirit is love, joy, peace, patience, kindness, goodness, faithfulness, gentleness, self-control (Gal. 5:22-23a. Cf. Matt. 7:22-23).

Again, Augustine noted many years ago the difficulty of the question of "proving" the Spirit's presence:

> In the earliest times, 'the Holy Ghost fell upon them that believed: and they spake with tongues,' which they had not learned, 'as the Spirit gave them utterance.' These were signs adapted to the time. . . . If then the witness of the presence of the Holy Ghost be not now given through these miracles, by what is it given, by what does one get to know that he has received the Holy Ghost? Let him question his own heart. If he love his brother, the Spirit of God dwelleth in him.[24]

When any specific physical sign is demanded as "proof" for a subjective experience, there will inevitably evolve an implicit "double-standard" that which will rigidly separate those who possess the sign from those who do not. Such has often been a stumbling block to Christian unity. Explicit in some Pentecostal writers is the view that Spirit-baptism—as objectified by glossolalia—is a prerequisite to sanctification.[25]

(3) In Christian worship there must be more opportunity for spontaneity—more avenues through which the worshippers may participate. Henry P. Van Dusen has concluded:

---

[23]Carl Brumback, *What Meaneth This? A Pentecostal Answer to a Pentecostal Question* (Gospel Publishing House, 1947), p. 266.

[24]Augustine, *Homilies on the First Epistle of John*, 6:10 in Philip Schaff (ed.), *Nicene and Post-Nicene Fathers* (first series 14 vols.; Eerdmans, 1956), 12:142.

[25]Cf. P. C. Nelson, *Bible Doctrines* (The Gospel Publishing House, 1948), p. 94 and Ralph M. Riggs, *The Spirit Himself* (Gospel Publishing House, 1949), p. 73.

> I have come to feel that the Pentecostal movement with its em-
> phasis upon the Holy Spirit, is more than just another revival.
> It is a revolution in our day. It is a revolution comparable in im-
> portance with the establishment of the original Apostolic
> Church and with the Protestant Reformation.[26]

It may be that one of the greatest needs of the modern church
is to rediscover the tremendous resources of the Holy Spirit.
All of Christendom needs to experience the joy and vigor of
the Spirit's presence. It was James McCord who said:

> Ours must become the Age of the Spirit, of God active in the
> world, shaking and shattering all our forms and structures,
> and bringing forth responses consonant with the gospel and
> the world's need.[27]

Could it be that through this "strange stirring in the Church"
God may be calling his "people back to a higher level of both
faith and practice."[28]

(4) The time has come for constructive dialog between the
glossolalists and non-glossolalists. Every Christian needs
both order and freedom. Out of constructive debate could
come a resolution of differences that would be profitable for
all.

CONCLUSION

Admittedly, many times glossolalia arises out of a highly
charged emotional atmosphere. Often those who speak in
tongues are ultra-conservative, and consequently one reaction
is to dismiss the entire movement as the product of some kind
of psychosis that comes to the surface during high-pitched re-

---

[26]Quoted in Sherrill, *They Speak with Other Tongues* (Revell, 1964),
p. 27.

[27]Quoted in ibid., p. 68.

[28]Russell T. Hitt, "The New Pentecostalism: An Appraisal," *Eternity*, 14 (July 1963): 10.

vivalist meetings. Such a cursory dismissal of the challenge of the glossolalists, however, does not settle the question: "What does this new 'outburst of tongues' signify for the rest of Christendom?"

From a non-glossolalist perspective, those who reject its form as no longer relevant for the church ought to be secure enough to concede that these random speech sounds that flow from the mouth of the glossolalist *may* attest to a genuine experience: namely, that God's Spirit is dwelling in the individual in power. The non-glossolalist—admitting that the symbol originally attested to the power and presence of God—is obligated to search elsewhere for a relevant symbol that may be used to indicate his commitment to the presence of the Spirit.

The proponents of glossolalia must recognize that the experience had been abused in the Corinthian congregation. Paul consequently set down some rules and limits for its future use. Of course, among the glossolalists in this century there have been similar abuses. The former General Secretary of the Pentecostal World Conference is reported to have said:

> There is not much in church services that is more distressing than the shocking ignorance about, and the lamentable absence of the gifts of the Holy Spirit. Even in our Pentecostal Churches, where there is evidence of more liberty in the Spirit, we find far more physical and emotional 're-actions' to the presence of the Spirit, than true manifestations of the gifts of the Spirit. . . . I consider it heresy to speak of shaking, trembling, falling, dancing, clapping, shouting, and such like actions as 'manifestations' of the Holy Spirit. These are purely human reactions to the power of the Holy Spirit and frequently hinder, more than help, to bring forth genuine manifestations.[29]

Consequently, those who speak in tongues need to recognize that these objections and fears are ever-present and real. The glossolalist must not expect all Christians to speak in tongues;

---

[29]Ewald, loc.cit.

neither must he deny his brother in Christ the right to search for other symbols to express the indwelling of God's Spirit, if that symbol would give concrete meaning to the conviction that God is dwelling in the individual in power.

The most important question about glossolalia for the church is this: Is glossolalia a legitimate expression of the presence of the Spirit? Paul would evidently answer this question in the affirmative—if the time and the place were "right." This would be determined by whether or not love is increased, or at the very least, not harmed in any way whatsoever. This will mean that both the glossolalists and the non-glossolalists alike will have to recognize that though their methods are different, their goal is the same: demonstrate the presence of God's Spirit. Regardless of the symbol, therefore, the gifts are to be judged: (1) the theological concerns and whether or not the lordship of Jesus is affirmed (1 Cor. 12:3; 1 John 1:1, 2:24, 4:2); and (2) the moral and practical test is made in light of the witness of the fruits (Matt. 7:15; Gal. 5:22-23), the Spirit of Christ (Rom. 8:9; 1 Cor. 13), and the usefulness to the church (1 Cor. 14:14-26).

BIBLIOGRAPHY

Abbott-Smith, G. *A Manual Greek Lexicon of the New Testament*. 3rd. ed. T. & T. Clark, 1937.

"Against Glossolalia," *Time*, 81 (May 18, 1963): 84.

Agrimson, J. Elmo, ed. *Gifts of the Spirit and the Body of Christ: Perspectives on the Charismatic Movement*. Augsburg, 1974.

Albertz, Martin D. *Die Botschaft des Neuen Testamentes*. Evangelischer Verlag, 1952.

Albright, William Foxwell. *From the Stone Age to Christianity*. 2nd. ed. John Hopkins Press, 1946.

Allen, Jimmy. "The Corinthian Glossolalia: The Historical Setting, An Exegetical Examination, and a Contemporary Restatement." Unpublished doctor's dissertation, Southwestern Baptist Theological Seminary, 1967.

Allen, Stuart. *Tongues Speaking Today: A Mark of Spirituality or Deception?* Berean Publishing Trust, 1971.

Alphandéry, Paul. "La glossolalie dans le prophétisme mediéval latin," *Revue d'historie des Religions*, 104 (November 1931): 417-36.

Amiot, F. "Glossolalie," *Catholicisme*, 5 (1962): 67-69.

Anderson, C. "Tongues of Men and Angels," *Lutheran Standard* (May 16, 1972): 6.

Andrews, Elias. "Ecstasy," *The Interpreter's Dictionary of the Bible*, George Arthur Buttrick, editor. 4 vols. Abingdon Press, 1962. A-D:21-22.

_____. "Tongues, Gift of," *The Interpreter's Dictionary of the Bible*, George Arthur Buttrick, editor. 4 vols. Abingdon Press, 1962. R-Z:671-72.

Ansons, Gunars. "The Charismatics and Their Churches: Report on Two Conferences," *Dialog*, 15:2 (1976): 142-44.

The Apocrypha of the Old Testament, Revised Standard Version. Thomas Nelson and Sons, 1957.

Arnot, Arthur B. "The Modern 'Speaking with Tongues,'" *The Evangelical Christian*, 46 (January 1950): 23-25, 59.

Arthur, William. *Tongues of Fire*. Harper and Brothers, 1856.

Ashcraft, Jessie Morris. "Glossolalia in the First Epistle to the Corinthians," in *Tongues*, Luther B. Dyer, editor. LeRoi Publishers, 1971. Pp. 60-84.

_____. "Speaking in Tongues in the Book of Acts," in *Tongues*, Luther B. Dyer, editor. LeRoi Publishers, 1971. Pp. 85-104.

Babbitt, Frank Cole (trans.). *Plutarch's Moralia*. "The Loeb Classical Library." 10 vols. William Heinemann, 1944-1949.

Bach, Marcus. *The Inner Ecstasy: The Power and Glory of Speaking in Tongues*. Abingdon Press, 1969.

_____. "Whether There Be 'Tongues,'" *Christian Herald*, 87 (May 1964): 10-11, 20, 22.

Bacon, B. W. "Professor Harnack on the Lukan Narrative," *American Journal of Theology*, 13 (1909): 59-76.

von Baer, Heinrich. *Der heilige Geist in den Lukasschriften*. Verlag von W. Kohlhammer, 1962.

Baer, Richard A. "Quaker Silence, Catholic Liturgy, and Pentecostal Glossolalia—Some Functional Similarities," in *Perspectives on the New Pentecostalism*, Russell F. Spittler, editor. Baker Book House, 1976. Pp. 150-64.

Baker, Cheryl Diane. "A Psycho-Political Comparison of Hallucinatory Phenomena Amongst Schizophrenics, LSD Users and Glossolalics." Unpublished master's thesis, University of Witwatersrand, 1983.

Baker, D. L. "An Interpretation of 1 Corinthians 12-14," *Evangelical Quarterly*, 46 (October-December 1974): 224-34.

Banks, R. J. and G. N. Moon. "Speaking in Tongues: A Survey of New Testament Evidence," *Churchman*, 80 (Winter 1966): 278-94.

Barde, E. "La Glossolalie," *Revue de théologie et des questions religieuses*, 5 (1896): 125-38.

Barnette, Maurice. *The Living Flame*. Epworth Press, 1953.

Barrett, C. K. *Luke the Historian in Recent Study*. Epworth Press, 1961.

Bartlet, Vernon. *The Acts*. Oxford University Press, 1902.

Bartling, V. A. "Notes on Spirit-Baptism and Prophetic Utterance," *Concordia Theological Monthly*, 39 (November 1968): 708-14.

Bartling, W. J. "Congregation of Christ: A Charismatic Body: An Exegetical Study of 1 Corinthians 12," *Concordia Theological Monthly*, 40 (February 1969): 67-80.

Barton, George A. *Archaeology and the Bible*. 7th. ed. American Sunday School Union, 1937.

Basham, Don. *A Handbook of Holy Spirit Baptism*. Whitaker Books, 1969.

_____. *A Manual for Spiritual Warfare*. Manna Books, 1974.

_____. "I Saw My Church Come to Life," *Christian Life*, 26 (March 1965): 37-39.

Baür, Walter. *A Greek-English Lexicon of the New Testament and Other Early Christian Literature*. Trans. William F. Arndt and F. Wilbur Gingrich. 4th rev. ed. University of Chicago Press, 1952.

Beare, Frank W. "Speaking With Tongues," *Journal of Biblical Literature*, 83 (September 1964): 229-46.

Beasley-Murray, George R. "Tongues-Speaking in the Ancient World," *Illustrator*, 5:3 (Spring 1979): 22-24.

Behm, Johannes. "γλῶσσα," *Theological Dictionary of the New Testament*, Gerhard Kittel, editor. Trans. Geoffrey W. Bromiley. 10 vols. Eerdmans, 1964-1976. 1:719-27.

Bell, Henry. "Speaking in Tongues." Unpublished doctor's dissertation, Evangelical Theological College, 1930.

Bellshaw, William G. "The Confusion of Tongues," *Bibliotheca Sacra*, 120 (April-June 1963): 145-53.

Benner, P. D. "The Universality of Tongues," *The Japan Christian Quarterly*, 39 (Spring 1973): 101-107.

Bennett, Dennis J. *Nine O'Clock in the Morning*. Logos International, 1970

_____. "Pentecost: When Episcopalians Start Speaking in Tongues," *The Living Church*, 142 (January 1, 1961): 12-13.

_____. "They Spake with Tongues and Magnified God!" *Full Gospel Business Men's Voice*, 8 (October 1960): 6-8.

_____. *When Episcopalians Start Speaking in Tongues*. Christian Retreat Center, n.d.

Bennett, Dennis and Rita Bennett. *The Holy Spirit and You*. Logos International, 1971.

Benson, Frank. "A Story of Division," in *The Charismatic Movement*, Michael Hamilton, editor. Eerdmans, 1975. Pp. 185-94.

Bergquist, Susan L. "The Revival of Glossolalic Practices in the Catholic Church: Its Sociological Implications," *Perkins Journal*, 30 (1973): 256-6

Bergsma, Stuart. *Speaking With Tongues: Some Physiological and Psychological Implications of Modern Glossolalia*. Baker Book House, 1965.

_____. "Speaking with Tongues," *Torch and Trumpet*, 14 (November 1964): 8-11.

_____. "Speaking with Tongues," *Torch and Trumpet*, 14 (December 1964): 9-13.

Bess, Donovan. "Speaking in Tongues—the High Church Heresy," *The Nation*, 197 (September 28, 1963): 173-77.

Best, Ernest. "The Interpretation of Tongues," *Scottish Journal of Theology*, 28:1 (1975): 45-62.

Bittlinger, Arnold. "Charismatic Renewal: An Opportunity for the Church," *The Ecumenical Review*, 31:3 (1979): 247-51.

_____. *The Church is Charismatic*. World Council of Churches, 1981

_____. "Et ils prient en d'autres langues: le movement charismatique et la glossolalie," *Foi et Vie*, 72:4 (1973): 97-108.

_____. "Gemeinde und Charisma," *Das nissionarische Wort*, 17 (1964) 231-35.

_____. *Gifts and Graces: A Commentary on 1 Corinthians 12-14*. Eerdmans, 1967.

_____. *Glossolalia: Wert und Problematik des Sprachenredens*. Kühne, 1969.

Bittlinger, Arnold and Kilian McDonnell. *Baptism in the Holy Spirit as an Ecumenical Problem*. Charismatic Renewal Services, Inc., 1972.

Black, Matthew. *An Aramaic Approach to the Gospels and Acts*. Clarendon Press, 1946.

Blaney, H. J. S. "Der Heilige Geist in der Pfingstbewegung und in der charismatischen Bewegung," in *Taufe und Heiliger Geist*, Pertti Mäki, editor. Helsinki, 1979. Pp. 89-105.

_____. "St. Paul's Posture on Speaking in Unknown Tongues," *Wesley Theological Journal*, 8 (1973): 52-60.

Blass, Friedrich. *Philology of the Gospels*. Macmillan and Company, 1898.

Blass, Friedrich and A. Debrunner. *A Greek Grammar of the New Testament and Other Early Christian Literature*. Trans. Robert W. Funk. Rev. ed. University of Chicago Press, 1961.

Bleek, F. "Noch ein Paar Worte über die Gabe ges γλώσσαις λαλεῖν," *Theologische Studien und Kritiken*, 3 (1830): 45-64.

_____. "Über die des γλώσσαις λαλεῖν in er ersten christlichen kirche," *Theologische Studien und Kritiken* (1829): 3-79.

Bloch-Hoell, Nils. "Der Heiligen Geist in der Pfingstbewegung und in der charismatischen Bewegung," in *Taufe und Heiligen Geist*, Pertti Mäki, editor. Helsinki, 1979. Pp. 89-105.

_____. *The Pentecostal Movement: Its Origin, Development, and Distinctive Character*. Allen and Unwin, 1964.

Bloesch, Donald G. "The Charismatic Revival," *Religion in Life*, 35 (Summer 1966): 364-80.

Blunt, A. W. F. *The Acts of the Apostles*, Clarendon Press, 1922.

Bobon, Jean. "Les Pseudo-Glossolalies Ludiques et Magiques," *Journal Belge de Neurologie et de Psychiatrie*, 47 (April 1947): 219ff.

Boer, Harry R. "The Spirit: Tongues and Message," *Christianity Today*, 7 (January 4, 1963): 6-7.

Boisen, Anton T. *Religion in Crisis and Custom: A Sociological and Psychological Study*. Harper & Row, 1955.

Bord, Richard J. and Joseph E. Faulkner. *The Catholic Charismatics: Anatomy of a Modern Religious Movement*. Pennsylvania State University Press, 1984.

Bosworth, Fred F. *Do All Speak With Tongues?* Christian Alliance Publishing Company, n.d.

Bover, P. "Le parler en langues des premiers chrétiens," *Revue d'histoire des religions*, 63 (1911): 292-310.

Brandt, R. L. "The Case for Speaking in Tongues," *Pentecostal Evangel*, 48 (June 5, 1960): 4, 29-30.

Breasted, James Henry. *Ancient Records of Egypt*. 5 vols. University of Chicago Press, 1906.

Breckenridge, James F. *The Theological Self-Understanding of the Catholic Charismatic Movement*. University Press of America, 1980.

Bredesen, Harald. "Discovery at Hillside," *Christian Life*, 20 (January 1959): 16-18.

_____. "Discovery at Yale," *Trinity*, 1 (Christmastide 1962-1963): 15-17.

Briggs, Charles. *New Light on the Life of Jesus*. Charles Scribner's Sons, 1904

_____. "The Use of 'ruach' in the Old Testament," *Journal of Biblical Literature*, 19 (1900): 132-45.

Broadbent, W. G. *The Doctrine of Tongues*. Eldon Press, n.d.

Broneer, Oscar. "Corinth," *The Biblical Archaeologist*, 16 (December 1951): 78-96.

_____. "Excavations in the Agora at Corinth," *American Journal of Archaeology*, 37 (1933): 554-72.

Brown, Francis, S. R. Driver and Charles Briggs. *A Hebrew and English Lexicon of the Old Testament*. Houghton Mifflin Company, 1907.

Brown, L. B. "Some Attitudes Surrounding Glossolalia," *Colloquim*, 2 (1967): 221-28.

Bruce, W. S. *The Ethics of the Old Testament*. T. & T. Clark, 1895.

Bruner, B. H. *Pentecost: A Renewal of Power*. Doubleday, Doran and Company, 1928.

Bruton, James Reed. "The Concept of the Holy Spirit as a Theological Motif in Luke-Acts." Unpublished doctor's dissertation, Southern Baptist Theological Seminary, 1967.

Bryant, Ernest, and Daniel O'Connell. "A Phonemic Analysis of Nine Samples of Glossolalic Speech," *Psychonomic Speech*, 22 (1971): 81-83.

Bultmann, Rudolf. *Theology of the New Testament*. Trans. Kendrick Grobel. 2 vols. SCM Press, 1955.

Bunn, John T. "Glossolalia in Historical Perspective," in *Speaking in Tongues: Let's Talk about It*, Watson E. Mills, editor. Word Books, 1973. Pp. 36-47.

Burgess, Stanley M. "Medieval Examples of Charismatic Piety in the Roman Catholic Church," in *Perspectives on the New Pentecostalism*, Russell P. Spittler, editor. Baker Book House, 1976. Pp. 14-26.

Burgess, W. J. *Glossolalia: Speaking in Tongues*. Baptist Publications Committee, 1968.

Burkitt, F. C. "Professor Torrey on Acts," *Journal of Theological Studies*, 20 (1918): 320-29.

Burrows, Millar. *More Light on the Dead Sea Scrolls*. The Viking Press, 1958.

Cadbury, Henry J. "Acts of the Apostles," *The Interpreter's Dictionary of the Bible*, George Arthur Buttrick, editor. 4 vols. Abingdon Press, 1962. A-D: 28-42.

_____. "The Macellum of Corinth," *Journal of Biblical Literature*, 53 (1934): 134-41.

_____. *The Style and Literary Method of Luke*, Parts I and II. Harvard University Press, 1920.

Callaway, Joseph A. "Corinth," *Review and Expositor*, 57 (October 1960): 381-88.

Campbell, J. A. "A Speaking Acquaintance With Tongues." Unpublished paper, University of Pittsburg, 1965.

Carpenter, Rhys. *Ancient Corinth*. American School of Classical Studies, 1954.

Carroll, R. Leonard. "Glossolalia: Apostles to the Reformation," in *The Glossolalia Phenomenon*, Wade H. Horton, editor. Pathway Press, 1966. Pp. 69-94.

Carter, Charles W. "A Wesleyan View of the Spirit's Gift of Tongues in the Book of Acts," *Wesleyan Theological Journal*, 4 (Spring 1969): 39-68.

Carver, William Owen. *The Acts of the Apostles*. Sunday School Board, Southern Baptist Convention, 1916.

Chafer, Lewis Sperry. "The Baptism of the Holy Spirit," *Bibliotheca Sacra*, 109 (1952): 199-216.

Charles, R. H. *The Apocrypha and Pseudepigrapha of the Old Testament in English*. 2 vols. Clarendon Press, 1913.

Christenson, Larry. *Speaking in Tongues and Its Significance for the Church*. Bethany, 1968.

Christie-Murray, David. *Voices from the Gods: Speaking with Tongues*. Routledge and Kegan Paul, 1978.

Clark, Stephen. *Baptized in the Spirit*. Dove Publications, 1970.

Clemens, Carl. "The 'Speaking With Tongues' of the Early Christians," *Expository Times*, 10 (1898): 344-52.

Cleveland, Lester. "Let's Demythologize Glossolalia," *The Baptist Program*, 45 (June 1967): 8, 11.

Cocoris, G. Michael. "Speaking in Tongues: Then and Now," *Biblical Research Quarterly*, 46:6 (September 1981): 14-16.

Coe, George Albert. *The Psychology of Religion*. University of Chicago Press, 1916.

Cohn, Werner. "A Movie of Experimentally-Produced Glossolalia," *Journal for the Scientific Study of Religion*, 6 (1967): 278.

_____. "Personality, Pentecostalism, and Glossolalia: A Research Note on Some Unsuccessful Research," *The Canadian Review of Sociology and Anthropology*, 5 (1968): 36-39.

"Concern Over Glossolalia," *Christianity Today*, 7 (May 24, 1963): 30.

Conn, Charles W. "Glossolalia and the Scriptures," in *The Glossolalia Phenomenon*, Wade H. Horton, editor. Pathway Press, 1966. Pp. 23-65.

Coulson, Jesse E. "Glossolalia and Internal-External Locus of Control," *Journal of Psychology and Theology*, 5:4 (1977): 312-17.

Craig, Clarence T. "Exegesis: The First Epistle to the Corinthians," *The Interpreter's Bible*, George Arthur Buttrick, editor. 12 vols. Abingdon Press, 1953. 10:14-276.

Cranfield, C. E. B. *A Commentary on Romans 12-13*. Oliver and Boyd, 1965.

Cross, James A. "Glossolalia: Its Value to the Church," in *The Glossolalia Phenomenon*, Wade H. Horton, editor. Pathway Press, 1966. Pp. 181-213.

Cullmann, Oscar. *Peter*. Westminster Press, 1953.

Culpepper, Robert H. *Evaluating the Charismatic Movement*. Judson Press, 1977.

_____. "Survey of Some Tensions Emerging in the Charismatic Movement," *Scottish Journal of Theology*, 30 (November 5, 1977): 439-52.

Currie, Stuart D. "Speaking in Tongues: Early Evidence Outside the New Testament Bearing on 'Glossais Lalein,'" *Interpretation*, 19 (1965): 274-94.

Cutten, George Barton. *The Psychological Phenomena of Christianity*. Scribner's Sons, 1908.

_____. *Speaking with Tongues: Historically and Psychologically Considered*. Yale University Press, 1927.

Dahl, N. A. "The Purpose of Luke-Acts" in *Luke and the Gnostics: An Examination of Lucan Purpose*. Abingdon Press, 1966. Pp. 87-98.

Dalton, Robert Chandler. *Tongues Like As of Fire*. Gospel Publishing House, 1945.

Dana, H. E. *The Holy Spirit in Acts*. Central Seminary Press, 1943.

Davies, Douglas. "Social Groups, Liturgy, and Glossolalia," *Churchman*, 90 (July-September 1976): 193-205.

Davies, J. G. "Pentecost and Glossolalia," *Journal of Theological Studies*, 3 (October 1952): 228-31.

Davies, W. D. *Paul and Rabbinic Judaism*. S. P. C. K., 1948.

Day, Charles L. "Glossolalia in Biblical and Post-Biblical Perspective." Unpublished doctor's dissertation, Golden Gate Seminary, 1971.

Dean, John Taylor. *St. Paul and Corinth*. Lutterworth Press, 1947.

Dean, Robert L. "Strange Tongues: A Psychologist Studies Glossolalia," *SK&F Psychiatric Reporter*, 14 (May-June 1964): 15-17.

Decker, Ralph Winefield. "The First Christian Pentecost." Unpublished doctor's dissertation, Boston University, 1941.

Deissmann, Adolf. *Light from the Ancient East*. Trans. Lionel R. M. Strachan. Hodder and Stoughton, 1910.

Dewar, Lindsay. The Holy Spirit and Modern Thought. A. R. Mowbray and Company, 1959.

_____. "The Problem of Pentecost," *Theology*, 9 (1924): 249-59.

Dhorme, Paul. "L'emploi métaphorique des noms de parties du corps en hébreu et en akkadien," *Revue Biblique*, 30 (1921): 517-40.

Diels, Hermann. *Die Fragmente der Vorsokratiker*. 2 vols. Weidmann, 1951-1952.

Dillistone, F. W. "The Biblical Doctrine of the Holy Spirit," *Theology Today*, 3 (1946-1947): 486-97.

Dirks, Lee E. "The Pentecostals: Speaking in Other Tongues," in *National Observer News Book: Religion in Action*. The National Observer, 1965. Pp. 168-76.

Dittenberger, Willhelm, ed. *Sylloge Inscriptionum Graearum*. 3 vols. 2nd. ed. Apud S. Hirzelium, 1888-1901.

Dodd, C. H. *The Bible and the Greeks*. Hodder and Stoughton, 1935.

Dodds, E. R. *The Greeks and the Irrational*. Beacon Press, 1951.

Dollar, George W. "Church History and the Tongues Movement," *Bibliotheca Sacra*, 120 (October-December 1963): 316-21.

Dominy, Bert. "Paul and Spiritual Gifts: Reflections on 1 Corinthians 12-14," *Southwestern Journal of Theology*, 26:1 (Fall 1983): 49-68.

Dorland, W. A. Newman. *The American Illustrated Medical Dictionary*. 21st. ed. W. B. Saunders Company, 1947.

Douglas, J. D. "Tongues in Transition," *Christianity Today*, 10 (July 8, 1966): 34.

Duewel, Wesley L. *The Holy Spirit and Tongues*. Light and Life Press, 1974

Dupont, Jacques. *Études sur les Actes des Apôtres*. Cerf, 1967.

_____. "Le Salut des Gentils et la Signification Theologique du Livre des Actes," *New Testament Studies*, 6 (1959-1960): 132-55.

_____. *The Sources of Acts*. Trans. Kathleen Pond. Darton, Longman and Todd, 1964.

Dyer, Luther B., ed. *Tongues*. LeRoi Publishers, 1971.

Eason, Gerald M. "The Significance of Tongues." Unpublished master's thesis, Dallas Theological seminary, 1959.

Easton, Burton Scott. "Tongues, Gift of," *The International Standard Bible Encyclopedia*. 5 vols. Howard-Severance Company, 1915. 5: 2995-97.

Edwards, Hubert E. "The Tongues at Pentecost: A Suggestion," *Theology*, 16 (1928): 248-52.

Edwards, O. C. "The Exegesis of Acts 8:4-25 and Its Implications for Confirmation and Glossolalia," *Anglican Theological Review*, supplementary series, no. 2 (September 1973): 100-12.

Ehrenstein, Herbert Henry. "Glossolalia: First Century and Today," *The King's Business* (November 1964): 31-34.

Eichrodt, Walther. *Theology of the Old Testament*. Trans. J. A. Baker. 2 vols. Westminster Press, 1961.

Eisenstein, J. D. "Pentecost in Rabbinic Literature," *The Jewish Encyclopedia*, Isidore Singer, editor. 12 vols. Funk and Wagnalls Company, 1906. 9: 592-94.

Elderen, Bastian van. "Glossolalia in the New Testament," *Bulletin of the Evangelical Theological Society*, 7 (Spring 1964): 53-58.

Eliade, Mircea. *Le chamanisme et les techniques archaïques de l'extase*. Payot, 1951.

_____. *Shamanism: Archaic Techniques of Ecstasy*. Trans. Willard R. Trask. Pantheon Books, 1964.

Ellis, E. Earle. "'Spiritual Gifts' in the Pauline Community," *New Testament Studies*, 20 (1974): 128-44.

Ellwood, Robert S., Jr. *One Way: The Jesus Movement and Its Meaning*. Prentice-Hall, 1973.

Engelsen, Nils Ivar Johan. "Glossolalia and Other Forms of Inspired Speech According to 1 Corinthians 12-14." Unpublished doctor's dissertation, Yale University, 1970.

Engelsviken, Tormod. "The Gift of the Spirit: An Analysis and Evaluation of the Charismatic Movement from a Lutheran Theological Perspective." Unpublished doctor's dissertation, Aquinas Institute, School of Theology, 1981.

Enslin, Morton Scott. *Christian Beginnings*. Harper and Brothers, 1938.

Erasmus, D. J. "Enkele Gedagtes oor Glossolalie," *Nederlands Theologisch Tijdschrift*, 12 (April 1971): 247-61.

Estes, Joseph Richard. "The Biblical Concept of Spiritual Gifts." Unpublished doctor's dissertation, Southern Baptist Theological Seminary, 1967.

Ewald, Tod W. "Aspects of Tongues," *The Living Church*, 146 (June 2, 1963): 12-13, 19.

_____. "Aspects of Tongues," *View*, 2:1 (1965): 7-11.

Failing, George E. "Should I Speak With Tongues," *The Wesleyan Methodist*, 122 (January 20, 1965): 6.

Faircloth, H. Rushton (trans.). *Virgil*. "The Loeb Classical Library." 2 vols. William Heinemann, 1922.

Farnell, L. R. *The Higher Aspects of Greek Religion*. William and Norgate, 1912.

Farrell, Frank. "Outburst of Tongues: The New Penetration," *Christianity Today*, 7 (September 13, 1963): 3-7.

Fee, Gordon. "Tongues—Least of the Gifts: Some Exegetical Observations on 1 Corinthians 12-14," *Pneuma*, 2:2 (Fall 1980): 3-14.

Feine, Paul. "Speaking with Tongues," *Schaff-Herzog Encyclopedia of Religious Knowledge*. 15 vols. Baker Book House, 1960. 11:36-39.

_____. "Zungenreden," *Realencyklopädie für protestantische Theologie und Kirch*. 24 vols. J. C. Hinrichs, 1908. 21:749-59.

Feine, Paul and Johannes Behm. *Introduction to the New Testament*, Werner Georg Kümmel, editor. Trans. A. J. Mattill. 14th rev. ed. Abingdon Press, 1966.

Ferguson, Charles W. *The Confusion of Tongues: A Review of Modern Isms*. Doubleday, Doran and Company, 1928.

Findlay, J. A. *The Acts of the Apostles: A Commentary*. Student Christian Movement Press, 1934.

Finegan, Jack. "Corinth," *The Interpreter's Dictionary of the Bible*, George Arthur Buttrick, editor. 4 vols. Abingdon Press, 1962. A-D: 682-84.

_____. *Light from the Ancient Past*. Princeton University Press, 1946.

Fink, Paul R. "The Phenomenon of Tongues as Presented in Scripture." Unpublished research paper, Dallas Theological Seminary, 1960.

Fisher, J. Franklin. *Speaking With Tongues*. Privately published, n.d.

Fisk, Samuel. *Speaking on Tongues in the Light of the Scripture*. The College Press, 1972.

Fison, J. E. *The Blessing of the Holy Spirit*. Longmans, Green, and Company, 1950.

Fleisch, D. Paul. *Die Pfingstbewegung in Deutschland*. Heinrich Feesche Verlag, 1957.

Flew, R. Newton. *Jesus and His Church*. Epworth Press, 1938.

Foakes-Jackson, F. J. and Kirsopp Lake. *The Beginnings of Christianity: The Acts of the Apostles*. 5 vols. Macmillan and Company, 1920-1933.

Ford, John T. "Tongues, Gift of," *The Encyclopedia Americana*. 30 vols. Americana Corporation, 1971. 26:839.

Forest, Tom. "Tongues: A Gift of Roses," *New Covenant*, 11:1 (July 1981): 15-17.

Fosbroke, Hughel. "The Prophetic Literature," *The Interpreter's Bible*, George Arthur Buttrick, editor. 12 vols. Abingdon Press, 1953. 1:201-11.

Fowler, J. Russell. "Holiness, the Spirit's Infilling, and Speaking with Tongues," *Paraclete*, 2 (Summer 1968): 7-9.

Fuller, Reginald H. "Tongues in the New Testament," *American Church Quarterly*, 3 (Fall 1963): 162-68.

Fusco, V. "Le sezioni-noi degli Atti nella discussione recente," *Bibliotheca Orientalis*, 25 (1983): 73-86.

Gaddis, Merle E. "Christian Perfectionism in America." Unpublished doctor's dissertation, University of Chicago, 1928.

Gæbelein, Arno C. "The So-Called Gift of Tongues," *Our Hope*, 14 (July 1907): 13-16.

Gæbelein, A. C. and F. C. Jennings. *Pentecostalism, the Gift of Tongues and Demon Possession*. Our Hope Publication Office, n.d.

Gasque, Ward W. *A History of the Criticism of the Acts of the Apostles*. Eerdmans, 1975.

Gee, Donald. "Do 'Tongues' Matter?" *Pentecost*, 49 (September 1958): 17.

_____. "Wheat, Tares and 'Tongues,'" *Pentecost*, 67 (December 1963-February 1964): 17.

Giesen, H. "Der Heilige Geist als Ursprung und treibende Kraft des christlichen Lebens. Zu den Geistaussagen der Apostelgeschichte," *Bibel und Kirche*, 37 (1982): 126-32.

Giles, K. "Salvation in Lukan Theology (2). Salvation in the Book of Acts," *Reformed Theological Review*, 42 (1983): 45-49.

Gillespie, Thomas W. "Pattern of Prophetic Speech in First Corinthians," *Journal of Biblical Literature*, 97 (March 1978): 74-95.

Ginns, R. "The Spirit and the Bride: St. Luke's Witness to the Primitive Church," *Life of the Spirit*, 12 (1957): 16-22, 58-64.

"Glossolalia," *The Living Church*, 146 (May 19, 1963): 11-12.

Glynne, W. "Psychology and Glossolalia: the Book of Acts," *Church Quarterly Review*, 106 (July 1928): 281-300.

Goguel, Maurice. *The Birth of Christianty*. Trans. H. C. Snape. Macmillan and Company, 1954.

Gonsalvez, Emma. "A Psychological Interpretation of the Religious Behavior of Pentecostals and Charismatics," *Journal of Dharma*, 7 (October-December 1982): 408-29.

_____. "The Theology and Psychology of Glossolalia." Unpublished doctor's dissertation, Northwestern University, 1978.

Goodman, Felicitas D. "The Acquisition of Glossolalia Behavior," *Semiotica*, 3 (1971): 77-82.

_____. "Altered Mental State vs. 'Style of Discourse': Reply to Samarin," *Journal for the Scientific Study of Religion*, 11 (1972): 297-99.

_____. "Disturbances in the Apostolic Church: Case Study of a Trance-Based Upheaval in Yucatan." Unpublished doctor's dissertation, Ohio State University, 1971.

_____. "Glossolalia and Hallucination in Pentecostal Congregations." Paper presented to the annual meeting of the American Anthropological Association, New York, 1971.

_____. "Glossolalia and Single-Limb Trance: Some Parallels," *Psychotherapy and Psychosomatics*, 19 (1971): 92-103.

_____. "Phonetic Analysis of Glossolalia in Four Cultural Settings," *Journal for the Scientific Study of Religion*, 8 (1969): 227-39.

_____. *Speaking in Tongues: A Cross-Cultural Study of Glossolalia*. University of Chicago Press, 1972.

_____. "Glossolalia: Speaking in Tongues in Four Cultural Settings," *Confinia Psychiatrica*, 12 (1969): 113-29.

Goodspeed, Edgar J., trans. *The New Testament: An American Translation*. University of Chicago Press, 1923.

_____. "The Origin of Acts," *Journal of Biblical Literature*, 39 (1920): 81-101.

Gosnell, L. W. "The Gift of Tongues: The True and the False," *The Christian Workers Magazine*, 13 (November 1913): 1-11.

Göttmann, Jacques. "La Pentecôte premices de la nouvelle crétion," *Bible et vie chrétienne*, 27 (1959): 59-69.

Goulder, M. D. *Type and History in Acts*. S. P. C. K., 1964.

"Government and Glossolalia," *Christianity Today*, 8 (July 31, 1964): 44-45.

"Government Grant for Study of 'Speaking in Tongues,'" *Pastoral Psychology*, 15 (September 1964): 53-54.

Grant, Frederick C. *The Gospels: Their Origin and Their Growth*. Harper & Row, 1957.

Grässer, Erich. "Die Apostelgeschichte in der Forschung der Gegenwart," *Theologische Rundschau*, 26 (1960-1961): 93-167.

Green, William M. "Glossolalia in the Second Century," *Restoration Quarterly*, 16 (1973): 231-39.

Greene, David. "The Gift of Tongues," *Bibliotheca Sacra*, 22 (January 1865): 99-126.

Grenfell, Bernard P., et al., eds. *The Oxyrhynchus Papyri*. 29 vols. Horace Hart, 1898-1963.

Griffiths, Michael F. *Three Men Filled with the Spirit: The Gift of Tongues*. Overseas Missionary Fellowship, 1969.

Gromacki, Robert Glenn. *The Modern Tongues Movement*. Presbyterian and Reformed Publishing Company, 1967.

Grudem, Wayne. "1 Corinthians 14:20-26: Prophecy and Tongues as Signs of God's Attitude," *Westminster Theological Journal*, 41 (Spring 1979): 381-96.

Grundmann, W. "Der Pfingstbericht der Apostelgeschichte in seinem theologischen Sinn," in *Studia Evangelica*, F. L. Cross, editor. Akademie-Verlag, 1964. Pp. 584-94.

Guillaume, Alfred. *Prophecy and Divination Among the Hebrews and Other Semites*. Hodder and Stoughton, 1938.

Gulledge, Jack. "Jibberish Is Not a Gift!" *Western Recorder*, 145 (January 2, 1971): 11.

Gundry, Robert H. " 'Ecstatic Utterance' (N.E.B.)?" *Journal of Theological Studies*, 17 (October 1969): 299-307.

Gutierrez, Lalei Elizabeth. "The Effects of Enhancement of Right Brain Functions Through Glossolalic Training on Nonverbal Sensitivity." Unpublished doctor's dissertation, Kent State University, 1980.

Haavil, O. L. "Pentecostalism or the Tongues Movement," *Lutheran Herald*, (October 23 and 30, 1934): 935-37, 959-63.

Hackett, Horatio B. *Commentary on the Original Text of the Acts of the Apostles*. Gould and Lincoln, 1858.

Haenchen, Ernst. *The Acts of the Apostles*. Westminster Press, 1971.

_____. "The Book of the Acts as Source Material for the History of Early Christianity," *Studies in Luke-Acts*, Leander E. Keck and J. L. Martyn, editors. Fortress, 1980. Pp. 259-66.

Haldeman, I. M. *Holy Ghost Baptism and Speaking with Tongues*. C. C. Cook, n.d.

Hall, Thor. "A New Syntax for Religious Language," *Theology Today*, 24 (July 1967): 172-84.

Hamman, Adalbert. "La nouvelle Pentecôte," *Bible et Vie Chrétienne*, 14 (1956): 82-90.

Hanson, James H. "A Personal Experience," in "Symposium on Speaking in Tongues," *Dialog*, 2 (Spring 1963): 152-53.

Hargrave, Vessie D. "Glossolalia: Reformation to the Twentieth Century," in *The Glossolalia Phenomenon*, Wade H. Horton, editor. Pathway Press, 1966. Pp. 97-139.

Harnack, Adolf von. *The Acts of the Apostles*. Trans. J. R. Wilkinson. Volume III of *New Testament Studies*. G. P. Putnam's Sons, 1909.

_____. *Luke the Physician*, W. D. Morrison, editor. Trans. J. R. Wilkinson. G. P. Putnam's Sons, 1907.

Harpur, T. W. "Gift of Tongues and Interpretation," *Canadian Journal of Theology*, 12 (July 1966): 164-71.

Harrison, Jane. *Prolegomena to the Study of Greek Religion*. Meridian Books, 1955.

Harrisville, Roy A. "Speaking in Tongues: A Lexicographical Study," *Catholic Biblical Quarterly*, 38 (January 1976): 35-48.

_____. "Speaking in Tongues: Proof of Transcendence?" *Dialog*, 13:1 (1974): 11-18.

Hayes, Doremus Almy. *The Gift of Tongues*. Jennings and Graham, 1913.

Haywood, Richard. "The Delphic Oracle," *Archaeology*, 5 (Summer 1952): 110-18.

Hegel, M. *Acts and the History of Earliest Christianity*. Trans. J. Bowden. Fortress Press, 1980.

Hendricks, William L. "Glossolalia in the New Testament," in *Speaking in Tongues: Let's Talk about It*, Watson E. Mills, editor. Word Books, 1973. Pp. 48-60.

Henke, Frederick G. "Gift of Tongues and Related Phenomena at the Present Day," *American Journal of Theology*, 13 (April 1909): 193-206.

Héring, Jean. *The First Epistle of Saint Paul to the Corinthians*. Trans. A. W. Heathcote and P. J. Allcock. Epworth Press, 1962.

Hilgenfeld, Adolf. *Die Glossolalie in der Alten Kirche*. Breitkopf und Härtel, 1850.

Hillis, Don W. *Tongues, Healing, and You*. Baker Book House, 1969.

_____. *What Can Tongues Do For You?* Moody Press, 1963.

Hine, Virginia. "Non-Pathological Pentecostal Glossolalia—A Summary of Psychological Literature." Unpublished report of the Pentecostal movement research committee, Department of Anthropology, University of Minnesota, 1967.

_____. "Pentecostal Glossolalia: Toward a Functional Interpretation," *Journal for the Scientific Study of Religion*, 8 (Fall 1969): 211-26.

Hinson, E. Glenn. "A Brief History of Glossolalia," in *Glossolalia: Tongue Speaking in Biblical, Historical, and Psychological Perspective*, Frank Stagg, E. Glenn Hinson, and Wayne E. Oates, editors. Abingdon Press, 1967. Pp. 45-75.

_____. "The Significance of Glossolalia in the History of Christianity," in *Speaking in Tongues: Let's Talk about It*, Watson E. Mills, editor. Word Books, 1973. Pp. 61-80.

Hobart, William Kirk. *The Medical Language of St. Luke*. Hodges, Figgs, and Company, 1882.

Hodges, Zane C. "The Purpose of Tongues," *Bibliotheca Sacra*, 120 (July-September 1963): 226-33.

Hoekema, Anthony. *Tongues and Spirit Baptism*. Baker Book House, 19??.

_____. *What About Tongue-Speaking?* Eerdmans, 1966.

Hoffman, James W. "Speaking in Tongues, 1963" *Presbyterian Life*, 16 (September 1, 1963): 14-17.

Holleaux, Maurice. *Etudes d'Epigraphie et d'Historie Grecques*. 3 vols. E. de Boccard, 1938-1942.

Hollenweger, Walter J. "Charismatische und pfingstlerische Bewegung als Frage an die Kirchen heute," in *Wiederentdeckung des Heiligen Geistes*. M. Lienhard and H. Meyer, editors. Lembeck, 1974. Pp. 53-76.

_____. *Enthusiastisches Christentum. Die Pfingstbewegung in Geschichte und Gegenwart*. Zwingli Verlag, 1969.

_____. "Literatur von und über die Pfingstbewegung (Weltkonferenzen, Holland, Belgien)," *Nederlands Theologisch Tijdschrift*, 18 (1963): 289-306.

_____. *The Pentecostals: The Charismatic Movement in the Churches.* Trans. R. A. Wilson. Augsburg, 1972.

_____. *Die Pfingskirchen: Selbstdarstellung Dokumente, Komentare.* Evangelisches Verlagswerk, 1971.

Holm, Lewis. "Speaking in Tongues," *The Lutheran Standard*, 2 (September 11, 1962): 3ff.

Holm, Nils G. "Functions of Glossolalia in the Pentecostal Movement," in *Psychological Studies on Religious Man*, Torvald Callstad, editor. Almkvist and Wiksell, 1978. Pp. 141-58.

Horn, William M. "Speaking in Tongues: A Retrospective Appraisal," *The Lutheran Quarterly*, 17 (November 1965): 316-29.

Horton, Wade. *What Is the Good of Speaking with Tongues?* Assemblies of God Publishing House, 1960.

House, H. Wayne. "Tongues and the Mystery Religions of Corinth," *Bibliotheca Sacra*, 140 (April-June 1983): 134-50.

Howe, Reuel. *The Miracle of Dialogue.* Seabury Press, 1963.

Hoyt, Herman. "Speaking in Tongues," *Brethren Missionary Herald*, 25 (1963): 156-57, 204-207.

Hughes, Ray H. "Glossolalia in Contemporary Times," in *The Glossolalia Phenomenon*, Wade H. Horton, editor. Pathway Press, 1966. Pp. 143-77.

Humphreys, Fisher and Malcolm Tolbert. *Speaking in Tongues.* Christian Litho, 1973.

Hunt, George L. *Speaking in Tongues.* Gospel Hall, n.d.

Hunter, Harold. "Tongue-Speech: A Patristic Analysis," *Journal of Evangelical Theological Society*, 23:2 (1980): 125-37.

Hutch, Richard A. "The Personal Ritual of Glossolalia," *Journal for Scientific Study of Religion*, 19:3 (1980): 255-66.

Inglis, James. "Gift of Tongues, Another View," *Theological Monthly*, 5 (1891): 425-27.

Isbell, Charles D. "Glossolalia and Propheteialalia: A Study of 1 Corinthi ans 14," *Wesley Theological Journal*, 10 (Spring 1975): 15-22.

Jacob, Edmond. *Theology of the Old Testament*. Trans. A. W. Heathcott and Philip J. Allcock. Harper and Brothers, 1958.

Jacobi, Walter. *Die Ekstase der alttestamentlichen Propheten*. J. F. Bergmann, 1920.

James, William. *The Varieties of Religious Experience*. Longmans, Green, ar Company, 1902.

Jamison, Leland. *Light for the Gentiles*. Westminster Press, 1961.

Jaquith, James R. "Toward a Typology of Formal Communicative Behav- ior: Glossolalia," *Anthropological Linguistics*, 9 (1967): 1-8.

Jaschke, Helmut. "Λαλεῖν bei Lukas," *Biblische Zeitschrift, neue folge*, 15:8 (1971): 109-14.

Jennings, George. "An Ethnological Study of Glossolalia," *Journal of the American Scientific Affiliation*, 20 (March 1968): 5-16.

Jervell, J. "The Acts of the Apostles and the History of Early Christianity *Studia Theologica*, 37 (1983): 17-32.

_____. *Luke and the People of God: A New Look at Luke-Acts*. Augsburg, 1972.

Jividen, Jimmy. *Glossolalia: From God or Man?* Star Publications, 1971.

Johanson, Bruce C. "Tongues, A Sign for Unbelievers? A Structural and Exegetical Study of 1 Corinthians 14:20-25," *New Testament Studies*, 25 (January 1979): 180-203.

Johnson, Aubrey R. *The Vitality of the Individual in the Thought of Ancient Is- rael*. University of Wales Press, 1949.

Johnson, S. Lewis. "The Gift of Tongues and the Book of Acts," *Bibliothec Sacra*, 120 (October-December 1963): 309-11.

Jones, Horace Leonard, trans. *The Geography of Strabo*. "The Loeb Classic Library." 8 vols. William Heinemann, 1927-1932.

Jones, W. H. S., trans. *Pausanias, Description of Greece*. "The Loeb Classic Library." 5 vols. Harvard University Press, 1918-1935.

Joyce, J. Daniel. "'Do All Speak With Tongues?'—No! 'Do Any Speak With Tongues?'—Maybe," *The Christian* (May 30, 1971): 678-79.

Jüngst, Johannes. *Die Quellen der Apostelgeschichte*. Friedrich Perathes, 1895.

Kaasa, Harris. "An Historical Evaluation," in "Symposium on Speaking in Tongues," *Dialog*, 2 (1963): 61-69.

Käsemann, Ernst. *Essays on New Testament Themes*. Trans. W. J. Montagne. Alec R. Allenson, 1964.

Kay, Thomas Oliver. "Pentecost: Its Significance in the Life of the Church." Unpublished master's thesis, Southern Baptist Theological Seminary, 1954.

Keiper, R. L. "Tongues and the Holy Spirit," *Moody Monthly*, 64 (September 1963): 61-69.

Kelsey, Morton T. *Tongue Speaking: An Experiment in Spiritual Experience*. Doubleday and Company, 1964.

Kendall, E. L. "Speaking With Tongues," *Church Quarterly Review*, 168 (January-March 1967): 11-19.

Kennedy, H. A. A. *St. Paul and the Mystery-Religions*. Hodder and Stoughton, 1913.

Kenyon, F. G. and H. I. Bell, eds. *Greek Papyri in the British Museum*. 5 vols. Oxford University Press, 1893-1917.

Kildahl, John P. "Psychological Observations," in *The Charismatic Movement*, Michael Hamilton, editor. Eerdmans, 1975. Pp. 124-42.

_____. *The Psychology of Speaking in Tongues*. Harper & Row, 1972.

Kildahl, John P. and Paul A. Qualben. "Final Progress Report: Glossolalia and Mental Health." Research project supported by the Behavioral Sciences Research Branch of the National Institute of Mental Health, 1971.

_____. "Relationships Between Glossolalia and Mental Health." A report of a study done on a grant from the Behavioral Sciences Research Branch of the National Institute of Mental Health, Bethesda, Maryland, 1971.

Killian, Matthew. "Speaking in Tongues," *The Priest*, 25 (November 1969): 611-16.

Knight, Harold. *The Hebrew Prophetic Consciousness*. Lutterworth Press, 1947.

Knox, W. L. *The Acts of the Apostles*. Cambridge University Press, 1948.

_____. *St. Paul and the Church of the Gentiles*. Cambridge University Press, 1939.

Koch, Kurt. *The Strife of Tongues*. Kregel Publications, 1969.

Korneman, Ernst and Paul M. Meyer, eds. *Griechische Papyri zu Giessen*. 3 vols. B. G. Teubner, 1910.

Krodel, Gerhard. "An Exegetical Examination," in "Symposium on Speaking in Tongues," *Dialog*, 2 (1963): 154-56.

Kucharsky, D. E. "Testing Tongues: Lutheran Medical Center Research Project," *Christianity Today*, 15 (June 4, 1971): 1-18.

Kümmel, Werner Georg. *Promise and Fulfilment*. SCM Press, 1957.

_____. "Das Urchristentum," *Theologische Rundschau*, 22 (1954): 191-211.

Kurz, W. S. "Hellenistic Rhetoric in the Christological Proof in Luke-Acts," *Catholic Biblical Quarterly*, 42 (1980): 171-95.

_____. "Luke-Acts and Historiography in the Greek Bible," *Society of Biblical Literature 1980 Seminar Papers*, Paul Achtemeier, editor. Scholars Press, 1980. Pp. 283-300.

Kuyper, Abraham. *The Work of the Holy Spirit*. Trans. Henri de Vries. Funk and Wagnalls Company, 1900.

Laffal, Julius, et al. "Communication of Meaning in Glossolalia," *Journal of Social Psychology*, 92 (April 1974): 277-91.

Lake, Kirsopp. *The Earlier Epistles of Paul*. Rivingtons, 1911.

Lampe, G. W. H. "The Holy Spirit in the Writings of St. Luke," *Studies in the Gospels*, D. E. Nineham, editor. Blackwell, 1955.

Landis, Carney and Marjorie M. Bolles. *Textbook of Abnormal Psychology*. Macmillan and Company, 1946.

Lapsley, James N. and John H. Simpson. "Speaking in Tongues: Infantile Babble or Song of the Self?" *Pastoral Psychology*, 15 (September 1964): 16-24.

_____. "Speaking in Tongues: Token of Group Acceptance and Divine Approval," *Pastoral Psychology*, 15 (May 1964): 48-55.

_____. "Speaking in Tongues," *Princeton Seminary Bulletin*, 58 (February 1965): 1-18.

Latte, Kurt. "The Coming of the Pythia," *The Harvard Theological Review*, 33 (1940): 9-18.

LeBarre, Weston. "Speaking in Tongues: Token of Group Acceptance and Divine Approval," *Pastoral Psychology*, 15 (May 1964): 48-55.

LeBarron, Albert. "A Case of Psychic Automation, Including 'Speaking With Tongues,'" *Proceedings of the Society for Psychical Research*, 12 (1896-1897): 277.

Lester, Andrew D. "Glossolalia: A Psychological Evaluation." Unpublished seminary paper, Southern Baptist Theological Seminary, 1965.

Lidsbarski, Mark. *Ephemeris für semitische Epigraphik*. 3 vols. J. Ricker, 1902-1915.

Lightner, Robert Paul. *Speaking in Tongues and Divine Healing*. Regular Baptist Press, 1965.

_____. *The Tongues Tide*. Empire State Baptist Fellowship, 1964.

Lillie, David George. *Tongues Under Fire*. Fountain Trust, 1966.

Lods, Adolphe. "Une tablette inedite de Mari, interessante pour l'historie ancienne du prophetisme semitique," *Studies in Old Testament Prophecy*, H. H. Rowley, editor. T. & T. Clark, 1950.

Lombard, Émile. *De la Glossolalie chez les premiers chrétiens et des phénomènes similaires*. G. Bridel. 1910.

_____. "Essai d'une classification des phénomènes de glossolalie," *Archives de Psychologie*, 7 (1908): 1-62.

Lovekin, Arthur Adams. "Glossolalia: A Critical Study of Alleged Origins, the New Testament and the Early Church." Unpublished master's thesis, University of the South, 1962.

Lovekin, Adams and Newton Malony. "Religious Glossolalia: A Longitudinal Study of Personality Changes," *Journal for the Scientific Study of Religion*, 16 (December 1977): 383-93.

Lowe, Harry W. *Speaking in Tongues: A Brief History of the Phenomenon Known as Glossolalia, or Speaking in Tongues*. Pacific Press Publishing Association, 1965.

Lumby, J. Rawson. *The Acts of the Apostles*. Cambridge University Press, 1912.

Lyonnet, S. "De glossolalia Pentecotes eiusque Significatione," *Verbum domini*, 24 (1944): 65-75.

Lyons, Bobbye. "Charismatic Gifts: An Exegesis of 1 Corinthians 12:1-11." Unpublished master's thesis, Columbia Theological Seminary, 1965.

MacDonald, Allan J. *The Interpreter Spirit and Human Life*. S. P. C. K., 194

MacDonald, William G. "Glossolalia in the New Testament," *Bulletin of the Evangelical Theological Society*, 7 (Spring 1964): 59-68.

_____. "The Place of Glossolalia in Neo-Pentecostalism," in *Speaking in Tongues: Let's Talk about It*, Watson E. Mills, editor. Word Books, 1973. Pp. 81-93.

McCasland, S. V. "Spirit," *The Interpreter's Dictionary of the Bible*, George Arthur Buttrick, editor. 4 vols. Abingdon Press, 1962. R-Z: 432-34.

McCrossan, T. J. *Speaking With Other Tongues: Sign or Gift—Which?* Christian Publications, 1919.

McGiffert, Arthur C. *A History of Christianity in the Apostolic Age*. Charles Scribner's Sons, 1897.

MacGorman, J. W. "Glossolalic Error and Its Correction: 1 Corinthians 12-14," *Review and Expositor*, 80:3 (Summer 1983): 389-400.

Macgregor, G. H. C. "Introduction and Exegesis," *The Interpreter's Bible*, George Arthur Buttrick, editor. 12 vols. Abingdon Press, 1953. 9: 1-35

Mackie, Alexander. *The Gift of Tongues*. George H. Doran Company, 192

McKinney, Joseph. "The Gift of Tongues: A School for Prayer and Ministry," *New Covenant*, 10:12 (June 1981): 12-15.

McNeile, A. H. *An Introduction to the Study of the New Testament*. 2nd. ed. Revised by C. S. C. Williams. Clarendon Press, 1955.

Maddox, R. *The Purpose of Luke-Acts*, Forschungen zur Religion und Literatur des Alten und Neuen Testaments 126. Vandenhoeck und Ruprecht, 1982.

Maeder, Alphonse. "La Langue d'un Aliéné: Analyse d'un Cas de Glossolalie," *Archives de Psychologie*, 9 (March 1910): 208-16.

Malony, H. Newton. "Debunking Some of the Myths About Glossolalia," *Journal of the American Scientific Affiliation*, 34:3 (September 1982): 144-48.

Malony, H. Newton, Nelson Zwaanstra, and James W. Ramsey. "Personal and Situational Determinants of Glossolalia: A Literature Review and Report of Ongoing Research." Paper presented at the International Congress of Religious Studies, Los Angeles, 1972.

Marcus, Ralph (trans). *Philo.* "The Loeb Classical Library." 10 vols. William Heinemann, 1939-1953.

Martin, Ira J. "1 Corinthians 13 Interpreted by Its Context," *The Journal of Bible and Religion*, 18 (April 1950): 101-105.

_____. "Glossolalia in the Apostolic Church," *Journal of Biblical Literature*, 63 (1944): 123-30.

_____. *Glossolalia in the Apostolic Church: A Survey Study of Tongue-Speech.* Berea College Press, 1960.

_____. "The Place of Significance of Glossolalia in the New Testament." Unpublished doctor's dissertation, Boston University, 1942.

Martin, R. A. "Syntactical Evidence of Aramaic Sources in Acts I-XV," *New Testament Studies*, 11 (1964): 38-59.

Mattill, A. J. and Mary Benford Mattill. *A Classified Bibliography of Literature on the Acts of the Apostles.* E. J. Brill, 1966.

May, Carlyle. "A Survey of Glossolalia and Related Phenomena in Non-Christian Religions," *American Anthropologist*, 58 (February 1956): 75-96.

Mayer, Marvin K. "The Behavior of Tongues," in *Speaking in Tongues: Let's Talk about It*, Watson E. Mills, editor. Word Books, 1973. Pp. 112-27.

_____. "The Behavior of Tongues," *Journal of the American Scientific Affiliation*, 23 (September 1971): 89-95.

Meeks, Fred E. "Pastor and the Tongues Movement," *Southwestern Journal of Theology*, 19 (Spring 1977): 73-85.

_____. "Pastoral Care and Glossolalia: Implications of the Contemporary Tongues Movement in American Churches." Unpublished doctor's dissertation, Southwestern Baptist Theological Seminary, 1976.

Mehl, Roger. "Approche sociologique des mouvements charismatiques," *Bulletin de la Société du Protestantisme Francais*, (octobre-novembre-décembre 1974): 555-73.

Mensbrugghe, Francoise van der. "Les Mouvements de Renouveau Charismatique. Retour de l'Esprit? Retour de Dionysos?" Unpublished dissertation, Université de Genève, 1978.

Methodists and the Baptism of the Holy Spirit. Full Gospel Business Men's Fellowship International, 1963.

Metz, Donald. *Speaking in Tongues: An Analysis*. Nazarene Publishing House, 1964.

Meyer, H. A. W. *Kritisch Exegetisches Handbuch über die Apostelgeschichte*. Vandenhoeck und Ruprecht, 1870.

Meyer, Johann A. G. *De charismatic* των γλωσσων praesertim Act. ii et I Cor. xiv. Lamminer, 1797.

Michael, John H. "The Gift of Tongues at Corinth," *The Expositor*, 4 (September 1907): 252-66.

Mills, Watson E. "Ecstaticism as a Background for Glossolalia," *Journal of the American Scientific Affiliation*, 27:4 (1975): 167-71.

_____. "Genesis of Glossolalia," *Averett Journal*, 4:2 (Fall 1972): 43-5

_____. "Glossolalia: Christianity's Counterculture Amidst a Silent Majority," *Christian Century*, 89 (September 27, 1972): 949-51.

_____. "Glossolalia: Creative Sound or Destructive Fury," *Home Missions*, 43 (August 1972): 8-13.

_____. "Glossolalia as a Socio-Psychological Experience," *Search*, 3 (Winter 1973): 46-53.

_____. "Glossolalia: A Study of Origins." Unpublished paper presented at the national meeting of the Society of Biblical Literature, Atlanta, October 29, 1971.

_____. "Glossolalia: The New Language of Zion," *People* (July 1973): 34-37.

_____. "Listening to the Glossolaliac: Going Beyond Words," *Western Recorder*, 145 (January 2, 1971): 10.

_____. "Literature on Glossolalia," *Journal of the American Scientific Affiliation*, 26:4 (December 1974): 169-73.

_____, ed. *Speaking in Tongues: Let's Talk about It*. Word Books, 1973.

_____. "Spiritual Gifts in the New Testament," *Illustrator*, 1:2 (Spring 1975): 29-33.

_____. "The Strange New Language of Christendom," in *The Lure of the Occult*, Watson E. Mills and M. Thomas Starkes, editors. Home Mission Board of the Southern Baptist Convention, 1974. Pp. 73-82.

_____. "A Theological Interpretation of Tongues in Acts and 1 Corinthians." Unpublished doctor's dissertation, Southern Baptist Theological Seminary, 1968.

_____. "Tongue Speech: Revolution or Renewal," *The Student*, 50 (November 1970): 29-31.

_____. *Understanding Speaking in Tongues*. Eerdmans, 1972.

Minear, Paul S. "Luke's Use of the Birth Stories," *Studies in Luke-Acts*, Leander E. Keck and J. Louis Martyn, editors. Abingdon Press, 1966. Pp. 111-30.

Moffatt, James. *The First Epistle of Paul to the Corinthians*. Harper and Brothers, 1933.

Moll, Albert. *Hypnotism*. Charles Scribner's Sons, 1913.

Montague, George T. "Baptism in the Spirit and Speaking in Tongues: A Biblical Appraisal," *Theology Digest*, 21 (1973): 342-60.

Montgomery, James A. "Hebrew *Hesed* and Greek *Charis*," *The Harvard Theological Review*, 32 (April 1959): 97-102.

Moody, Dale. *The Spirit of the Living God*. The Westminster Press, 1968.

Moorehead, William G. "Tongues of Fire," *The International Standard Bible Encyclopedia*. 5 vols. Howard-Severance Company, 1915. 5:2843-44.

_____. "Tongues of Fire," *International Standard Bible Encyclopedia*. 5 vols. The Howard-Severance Company, 1915. 5:2997-98.

Morentz, Paul. "Lecture on Glossolalia." Unpublished paper, University of California, 1966.

Morgenthaler, Robert. *Statistik des Neutestamentlichen Wortschatzes*. Gotthelf-Verlag, 1958.

Morris, Fred B. "Now I Want You All To Speak in Tongues," *The Christian Advocate*, 7 (July 4, 1963): 9-10.

Morton, A. Q. and G. H. C. Macgregor. *The Structure of Luke and Acts*. Hodder and Stoughton, 1964.

Mosiman, Eddison. *Das Zungenreden geschichtlich und psychologisch untersucht*. J. C. B. Mohr, 1911.

Motley, Michael T. "Glossolalia: Analyses of Selected Aspects of Phonology and Morphology." Unpublished master's thesis, University of Texas, 1967.

Mowinckel, Sigmund. " 'Spirit' and 'the Word' in the Pre-Exilic Reforming Prophets," *Journal of Biblical Literature*, 53 (1934): 199-227.

Mueller, Theodore. "A Linguistic Analysis of Glossolalia," *Concordia Theological Monthly*, 45:3 (July 1981): 186-91.

Neely, B. G. *Bible Versus the Tongues Theory*. Nazarene Publishing House, n.d.

Neff, H. Richard. "The Cultural Basis for Glossolalia in the Twentieth Century," in *Speaking in Tongues: Let's Talk about It*, Watson E. Mills, editor. Word Books, 1973. Pp. 26-35.

Nelson, J. Robert. *The Realm of Redemption*. Wilcox and Follett Company, 1951.

Ness, William H. "Glossolalia in the New Testament," *Concordia Theological Monthly*, 32 (April 1961): 221-23.

Newport, John P. "Speaking in Tongues," *Home Missions*, 36 (May 1965): 7-9, 21-26.

Nida, Eugene A. "Glossolalia: A Case of Pseudo-Linguistic Structure." Unpublished paper delivered at the 39th Annual Meeting of the Linguistic Society of America, New York City, December 28, 1964.

_____. "Preliminary Report on Glossolalia." A paper presented at the Linguistic Society of America, New York, 1964.

Niesz, Nancy L. and Earl J. Kronenberger. "Self-Actualization in Glossolalic and Non-Glossolalic Pentecostals," *Sociological Analysis: A Journal in the Sociology of Religion*, 39 (Fall 1978): 250-56.

Nietzsche, Friedrich. *The Birth of Tragedy*. Trans. Francis Golffing. Doubleday Anchor Books, 1956.

Northrup, Bernard E. *What You Should Know About . . . Tongues and Spiritual Gifts*. San Francisco Baptist Theological Seminary, n.d.

"Notes on Recent Exposition," *Expository Times*, 78 (May 1966): 225-27.

Nuttall, Geoffrey. "Spirit of Power and Love," *Interpretation*, 4 (1950): 24-35.

Wayne E. Oates. "Ecstaticism." Unpublished seminar paper, Duke University, 1943.

_____. "The Holy Spirit and the Overseer of the Flock," *Review and Expositor*, 63 (Spring 1966): 187-97.

_____. "A Socio-Psychological Study of Glossolalia," in *Glossolalia: Tongue Speaking in Biblical, Historical, and Psychological Perspective*, Frank Stagg, E. Glenn Hinson, and Wayne E. Oates, editors. Abingdon Press, 1967. Pp. 76-99.

Oates, Whitney J. and Eugene O'Neill, eds. *The Complete Greek Drama*. 2 vols. Random House, 1938.

O'Connell, Daniel C. and Ernest T. Bryant. "Some Psychological Reflections on Glossolalia," *Review for Religious*, 31 (1972): 174-77.

Oesterreich, T. K. *Possession: Demonical and Other*. Richard R. Smith, 1930.

Oliver, H. H. "The Lukan Birth Stories and the Purpose of Luke-Acts," *New Testament Studies*, 10 (1963): 202-26.

Olshausen, Hermann. *Biblical Commentary on the Gospels and on the Acts of the Apostles*. 4 vols. T. & T. Clark, 1847-1850.

Oman, John D. "On 'Speaking in Tongues': A Psychological Analysis," *Pastoral Psychology*, 14 (December 1963): 48-51.

O'Neill, J. C. *The Theology of Acts in Its Historical Setting*. SPCK, 1970.

Osser, H. A., et al. "Glossolalic Speech from a Psycholinguistic Perspective," *Journal of Psycholinguistic Research*, 2 (1973): 9-19.

Palma, Anthony D. "Glossolalia in the Light of the New Testament and Subsequent History." Unpublished bachelor's thesis, Biblical Seminary, 1960.

Palmer, Everett W. "Speaking in Tongues," *Christian Advocate*, 8 (October 22, 1964): 9-10.

Palmer, Gary. "Studies of Tension Reduction in Glossolalia." Unpublished paper, University of Minnesota, 1966.

Panton, D. M. *Irvingism, Tongues, and the Gifts of the Holy Ghost*. Charles J. Thynne and Jarvis, n.d.

Parke, H. W. and D. E. W. Wormell. *The Delphic Oracle*. 2 vols. Blackwell, 1956.

Pattison, E. Mansell. "Behavioral Research on the Nature of Glossolalia," *Journal of the American Scientific Affiliation*, 20 (September 1968): 73-86

_____. "Speaking in Tongues and About Tongues," *Christian Standard*, 98 (February 15, 1964): 1-2.

Pattison, E. Mansel and Robert L. Casey. "Glossolalia: A Contemporary Mystical Experience," in *Clinical Psychiatry and Religion*, E. Mansell Pattison, editor. Little, Brown and Company, 1968. Pp. 133-48.

_____. "Glossolalia: A Contemporary Mystical Experience," *International Psychiatry Clinics*, 5 (1969): 133-48.

_____. "Ideological Support for the Marginal Middle Class: Faith Healing and Glossolalia," in *Religious Movements in Contemporary America*, Irving I. Zaretsky and Mark P. Leone, editors. Princeton University Press, 1974.

Pavelsky, Robert L. "The Psychological Correlates of Act and Process Glossolalia as a Function of Socioeconomic Class, Expectation of Glossolalia, and Frequency of Glossolalic Utterance." Unpublished doctor's dissertation, Fuller Theological Seminary, Pasadena, 1975.

Pedersen, Johannes. *Israel, Its Life and Culture*. 4 vols. Oxford University Press, 1947.

Pfeiffer, Robert H. *Introduction to the Old Testament*. Harper and Brothers, 1941.

Pfister, Oskar. "Die psycologische Enträtselung der Religiösen Glossolalie und der automatischen Kryptographie," *Jahrbuch für psychoanalytische und psychopathologische Forschungen*, 3 (1912): 427ff.

Pierce, Flora M. Johnson. "Glossolalia," *Journal of Religion and Psychical Research*, 4 (July-October 1981): 168-78.

Pierson, A. T. *Speaking with Tongues*. Gospel Publishing House, n.d.

_____. "Speaking with Tongues," *Missionary Review*, 20 (1907): 487, 682.

Pike, James A. "Pastoral Letter Regarding 'Speaking in Tongues,'" *Pastoral Psychology*, 15 (May 1964): 56-61.

Pinnock, Clark H. and Grant R. Osborne. "A Truce Proposal for the Tongues Controversy," *Christianity Today*, 16 (October 8, 1971): 6-9.

Plog, Stanley C. "Preliminary Analysis of Group Questionnaires on Glossolalia." Unpublished data, University of California, 1966.

_____. "UCLA Conducts Research on Glossolalia," *Trinity*, 3 (Whitsuntide 1964): 38-39.

Plümacher, E. "Acta-Forschung 1974-1982," *Theologische Rundschau*, 48 (1983): 1-56.

Pope, R. Martin. "Gift of Tongues," *A Dictionary of the Apostolic Church*, James Hastings, editor. 2 vols. Charles Scribner's Sons, 1908. 1:598-99.

Poythress, Vern S. "Linguistic and Sociological Analyses of Modern Tongues-Speaking: Their Contributions and Limitations," *Westminster Theological Journal*, 42:2 (1980): 367-88.

Pratt, James B. *The Religious Consciousness*. Macmillan and Company, 1937.

"Preliminary Report, Study Commission on Glossolalia." Division of Pastoral Services, Diocese of California, May 2, 1963.

Preus, Klemet. "Nature of Glossolalia: Possible Options," *Westminster Theological Journal*, 40 (Fall 1977): 130-35.

_____. "Tongues: An Evaluation From a Scientific Perspective," *Concordia Theological Quarterly*, 46:4 (October 1982): 277-93.

Prince, Morton. *The Unconscious: The Fundamentals of Known Personality, Normal and Abnormal*. Macmillan and Company, 1913.

Pritchard, James B. *Ancient Near Eastern Texts*. Princeton University Press, 1950.

"Protestant Episcopal Church in the U.S.A. Diocese of California." Division of Pastoral Services, Study Commission on Glossolalia, May 2, 1963.

Putnam, W. G. "Tongues, Gift of," *New Bible Dictionary*, J. D. Douglas, editor. Eerdmans, 1962. Pp. 1286-87.

Quebedeaux, Richard. *The New Charismatics: The Origins, Development and Significance of Neo-Pentecostalism*. Doubleday and Company, 1976.

Rackham, R. B. *The Acts of the Apostles*. Methuen and Company, 1951.

von Rad, Gerhard. *Old Testament Theology*. Trans. D. M. G. Stalker. 2 vols. Oliver and Boyd, 1965.

Ramm, Bernard. *A Study of Some Special Problems in Reference to the Speaking in Tongues*. Bible Institute of Los Angeles, 1947.

_____. "The Word on Speaking in Tongues," *National Catholic Reporter*, 3 (April 26, 1967): 4.

Ramsay, W. M. "Luke the Physician," *Luke the Physician and Other Studies in the History of Religion*. Hodder and Stoughton, 1908.

Rarick, William John. "The Socio-Cultural Context of Glossolalia: A Comparison of Pentecostal and Neo-Pentecostal Religious Attitudes and Behavior." Unpublished doctor's dissertation, Fuller Theological Seminary, 1982.

Rawlinson, A. E. J. *The New Testament Doctrine of the Christ*. Longmans, Green, and Company, 1926.

"Report of the Field Study Committee on Speaking in Tongues." Commission on Evangelism of the American Lutheran Church, 1972.

"Report of the Special Commission on Glossolalia." To the Right Reverend Gerald Francis Burrill, Bishop of Chicago, December 12, 1960.

"Report on Glossolalia." A report of the Commission on Evangelism of the American Lutheran Church, Minneapolis, 1962.

Rice, John R. *Speaking With Tongues*. Sword of the Lord Publishers, 1970.

Rice, Robert F. "Christian Glossolalia Through the Centuries," *View*, 1 (1964): 1-7.

Richardson, James T. "Psychological Interpretations of Glossolalia: A Reexamination of Research," *Journal for the Scientific Study of Religion*, 12 (1973): 199-207.

Richardson, James T. and M. T. V. Reidy. "Form and Fluidity into Contemporary Glossolalic Movements," *The Annual Review of the Social Sciences of Religion*, 4 (1980): 183-220.

Richet, Charles. "Xenoglossie: l'écriture automatique en langues étrangères," *Proceedings of the Society for Psychical Research*, 19 (1905-1907): 162-94.

Righter, James D. "A Critical Study of the Charismatic Experience of Speaking in Tongues." Unpublished doctor's dissertation, Wesley Theological Seminary, 1974.

Roberts, Oral. *The Baptism With the Holy Spirit and the Value of Speaking in Tongues Today*. Privately published, 1964.

Robertson, Archibald and Alfred Plummer. *A Critical and Exegetical Commentary on the First Epistle of St. Paul to the Corinthians*. 2nd. ed. Charles Scribner's Sons, 1925.

Robertson, A. T. *A Grammar of the Greek New Testament in the Light of Historical Research*. George H. Doran Company, 1915.

_____. *Luke the Historian in the Light of Research*. Charles Scribner's Sons, 1920.

Robertson, Carl F. "The Nature of New Testament Glossolalia." Unpublished doctor's dissertation, Dallas Theological Seminary, 1975.

Robertson, O. Palmer. "Tongues: Sign of Covenantal Curse and Blessing," *Westminster Theological Journal*, 38:1 (1975): 43-53.

Robinson, H. Wheeler. "Holy Spirit in the Old Testament," *Encyclopedia Britannica*. 23 vols. William Benton, 1962. 11:686.

_____. *Inspiration and Revelation in the Old Testament*. Clarendon Press, 1946.

Robinson, James and Helmut Koester. *Trajectories through Early Christianity*. Fortress Press, 1971.

Robinson, Theodore H. *Prophecy and the Prophets*. Gerald Duckworth and Company, 1956.

Robinson, Wayne A. *I Once Spoke in Tongues*. Forum House Publishers, 1973.

Roddy, Andrew Jackson. *Though I Spoke With Tongues: A Personal Testimony*. The Harvester, 1952.

Roehrs, Stephen Paul. "Glossolalia Phenomena." Unpublished master's thesis, Concordia Theological Seminary, 1971.

Rogers, Cleon L. "The Gift of Tongues in the Post Apostolic Church," *Bibliotheca Sacra*, 122 (April-June 1965): 134-43.

Rohde, Erwin. *Psyche*. Harcourt, Brace and Company, 1925.

Rowley, H. H. *The Biblical Doctrine of Election*. Lutterworth Press, 1950

Royce, Josiah. *William James, and Other Essays on the Philosophy of Life*. Macmillan and Company, 1911.

Ruble, Richard Lee. "A Spiritual Evaluation of Tongues in Contemporar Theology." Unpublished doctor's dissertation, Dallas Theologica Seminary, 1964.

Runia, K. "Glossolalia as Learned Behavior," *Canadian Journal of Theology* 15 (1969): 60-64.

_____. "Speaking in Tongues in the New Testament," *Vox Reformata* (May 1965): 20-29, 38-46.

Saake, H. "Paulus als Ekstatiker: Pneumatologische Beobachtungen zu Corinthians 12:1-10," *Biblica*, 53:3 (1972): 404-10.

_____. "Pneumatologia Paulina: zur Katholizität der Problematik c Charisma," *Catholica*, 26:3 (1972): 212-23.

Sadler, A. W. "Glossolalia and Possession: An Appeal to the Episcopal Study Commission," *Journal for the Scientific Study of Religion*, 4 (1964): 84-90.

Samarin, William J. "Evolution in Glossolalic Private Language," *Anthro pological Linguistics*, 13 (1971): 55-67.

_____. "Glossolalia as Learned Behavior," *Canadian Journal of Theology*, 15 (1969): 60-64.

_____. "Glossolalia as Learned Behavior." Unpublished paper pre sented to annual meeting of the Society for Scientific Study of Religio Montreal, 1968.

_____. "Glossolalia as Regressive Speech," *Language and Speech*, 16 (1973): 77-89.

_____. "Glossolalia as Regressive Speech." Unpublished paper pre sented at the Meeting of the Linguistic Society of America, Columbu Ohio, 1970.

_____. "Glossolalia as a Vocal Phenomenon," in *Speaking in Tongues Let's Talk about It*, Watson E. Mills, editor. Word Books, 1973. Pp. 128-42.

_____. "The Glossolalist's 'Grammar of Use.'" Paper given at the Annual Meeting of the American Anthropological Association, San Diego, 1970.

_____. "The Linguisticality of Glossolalia," *The Hartford Quarterly*, 8 (1968): 49-75.

_____. "Sociolinguistic Versus Neurophysiological Explanations for Glossolalia: Comment on Goodman's Paper," *Journal for the Scientific Study of Religion*, 11 (Spring 1972): 293-99.

_____. *Tongues of Men and Angels: The Religious Language of Pentecostalism*. Macmillan and Company, 1972.

_____. "Variation and Variables in Religious Glossolalia," *Language in Society*, 1 (1972): 121-30.

Sassaman, Marcus B. "An Investigation of the Interpretations of Glossolalia." Unpublished bachelor's thesis, Western Evangelical Seminary, 1966.

Schaff, Philip, ed. *Ante-Nicene Fathers*. 10 vols. Charles Scribner's Sons, 1908.

_____. *History of the Christian Church*. 8 vols. Charles Scribner's Sons, 1882-1910.

_____. *Nicene and Post-Nicene Fathers*. Second series. 14 vols. Eerdmans, 1956.

Schlauch, Margaret. *The Gift of Tongues*. Modern Age Books, 1942.

Schoemaker, William R. "The Use of רוּחַ in the Old Testament and of πνεῦμα in the New Testament: A Lexicographical Study," *Journal of Biblical Literature*, 23 (1904): 13-67.

Schoeps, H. J. *Paul*. Trans. Harold Knight. Lutterworth Press, 1961.

Schweizer, Edward. *Spirit of God*. Trans. A. E. Harvey. Volume III, Part II of *Bible Key Words* from Gerhard Kittel (ed.), *Theologisches Wörterbuch zum Neuen Testament*. Harper and Brothers, 1961.

_____. "The Spirit of Power," *Interpretation*, 6 (1952): 259-78.

Scott, C. A. Anderson. "Christ, Christology," *A Dictionary of the Apostolic Church*, James Hastings, editor. 2 vols. Charles Scribner's Sons, 1908. 1:177-99.

Scott, Walter. *Hermetica*. 4 vols. Clarendon Press, 1924-1936.

Scroggie, W. Graham. *The Baptism of the Holy Spirit and Speaking With Tongues*. Marshall, Morgan, and Scott, n.d.

_____. *Speaking With Tongues*. Book Stall, 1919.

Seddon, A. E. "Edward Irving and Unknown Tongues," *Homiletic Review* 57 (1957): 103.

Sherill, John L. *They Speak With Other Tongues*. McGraw-Hill Book Company, 1964.

Shepherd, Massey H., ed. *The Oxford American Prayer Book Commentary*. Oxford University Press, 1950.

Shuler, R. P. *McPhersonism: A Study of Healing Cults and Modern Day Tongue Movements*. Privately published, 1924.

Shepherd, Massey H. (ed.). *The Oxford American Prayer Book Commentary* Oxford University Press, 1950.

Shumway, Charles William. "A Critical History of Glossolalia." Unpublished doctor's dissertation, Boston University, 1919.

Siirala, Aarne. "A Methodological Proposal," in "Symposium on Speaking in Tongues," *Dialog*, 2 (1963): 158-59.

Simmons, J. P. *History of Tongues*. Privately published, n.d.

Sirks, G. J. "The Cinderella of Theology: The Doctrine of the Holy Spirit, *The Harvard Theological Review*, 50 (1957): 77-89.

Skinner, John. *Prophecy and Religion*. Cambridge University Press, 192

Slay, James L. "Glossolalia: Its Value to the Individual," in *The Glossolalia Phenomenon*, Wade H. Horton, editor. Pathway Press, 1966. Pp. 217

Smith, B. L. "Tongues in the New Testament," *Churchman*, 87 (Winter 1973): 283-88.

Smith, Charles Russell. "Biblical Conclusions Concerning Tongues." Unpublished doctor's dissertation, Grace Theological Seminary, 1970

Smith, D. Moody. "Glossolalia and Other Spiritual Gifts in a New Testament Perspective," *Interpretation*, 28 (July 1974): 307-20.

Smith, Daniel Stephen. "Glossolalia: The Personality Correlates of Conventional and Unconventional Subroups." Unpublished doctor's dissertation, Rosemead Graduate School of Professional Psychology, 1977.

Smith, Karl Ludwig. *The Church*. Trans. J. R. Coates. Volume I, Part II of *Bible Key Words* from Gerhard Kittel, editor, *Theologisches Wörterbuch zum Neuen Testament*. Harper and Brothers, 1961.

Smylie, James H. "Testing the Spirits in the American Context: Great Awakenings, Pentecostalism, and the Charismatic Movements," *Interpretation*, 33:1 (1979): 32-46.

Snaith, Norman. *The Distinctive Ideas of the Old Testament*. Epworth Press, 1944.

_____. "The Spirit of God in Jewish Thought," *The Doctrine of the Holy Spirit*, Vincent Taylor, et al, compilers. Epworth Press, 1937.

Snyder, Dean J. "Confessions of a Closet Charismatic," *Christian Century*, 100 (May 1983): 878-81.

Speer, Blanche C. "A Linguistic Analysis of a Corpus of Glossolalia." Unpublished doctor's dissertation, University of Colorado at Boulder, 1971.

Spitta, Friedrich. *Die Apostelgeschichte: Thre Quellen und deren qeschichtlicher Wert*. Vandenhoeck und Ruprecht, 1891.

Spoerri, Theodore. "Ekstatische Rede und Glossolalie," in *Beiträge zur Ekstase*. Karger, 1967.

Stacey, W. D. *The Pauline View of Man*. Macmillan and Company, 1956.

Stagg, Frank. *The Book of Acts*. Broadman Press, 1955.

_____. "Glossolalia in the New Testament," in *Glossolalia: Tongue Speaking in Biblical, Historical, and Psychological Perspective*, Frank Stagg, E. Glenn Hinson, and Wayne E. Oates, editors. Abingdon Press, 1967. Pp. 20-44.

_____. "The Holy Spirit in the New Testament," *Review and Expositor*, 63 (Spring 1966), 135-49.

Stanley, Arthur P. "The Gift of Tongues and the Gift of Prophesying," in *A Collection of Theological Essays from Various Authors*, George R. Noyes, compiler. William Crosby, 1856. Pp. 453-71.

Stanley, Gordon, et al. "Some Characteristics of Charismatic Experience: Glossolalia in Australia," *Journal for the Scientific Study of Religion*, 17 (Spring 1978): 269-77.

"A Statement with Regard to Speaking in Tongues," in *Reports and Actions of the Second General Convention of the American Lutheran Church*, 1964.

Steadman, J. M. "Anent the Gift of Tongues and Kindred Phenomena," *Methodist Quarterly Review*, 74 (October 1925): 688-715.

Stegall, Carroll, Jr. *The Modern Tongues and Healing Movement*. Privately published, n.d.

Steinmetz, David. "Religious Ecstasy in Staupitz and the Young Luther," *The Sixteenth Century Journal*, 11:1 (1980): 23-37.

Stemme, Harry A. *Speaking with Other Tongues: Sign and Gift*. Northern Gospel Publishing House, 1946.

Stendahl, Krister. "Biblical Theology, Contemporary," *The Interpreter's Dictionary of the Bible*, George Arthur Buttrick, editor. 4 vols. Abingdon Press, 1962. A-D: 418-32.

_____. "The New Testament Evidence," in *The Charismatic Movement*, Michael Hamilton, editor. Eerdmans, 1975. Pp. 49-60.

Sterrett, T. Norton. "The New Testament Charismata." Unpublished doctor's dissertation, Dallas Theological Seminary, 1947.

Stevenson, Ian. *Xenoglossy*. University of Virginia Press, 1974.

Stibbs, A. M. "Putting the Gift of Tongues in Its Place," *The Churchman*, 80 (Winter 1966): 295-303.

Stolee, Haakon J. *Speaking in Tongues*. Augsburg, 1963.

Strack, Hermann L. and Paul Billerbeck. *Kommentar zum Neuen Testament aus Talmud und Midrasch*. 6 vols. Beck, 1922-1961.

Streeter, B. H. *The Four Gospels: A Study of Origins*. Macmillan and Company, 1924.

_____. *The God Who Speaks*. Macmillan and Company, 1936.

Stringer, Randy C. *What the Bible Teaches About the Purpose of Tongue Speaking*. Privately published, 1971.

Suenens, Leon. *A New Pentecost*. Trans. Francis Martin. Seabury Press, 1973.

Sullivan, Francis A. "Speaking in Tongues," *Lumen Vitae*, 31:2 (1976): 145-70.

Summers, Ray. "Unknown Tongues: 1 Corinthians 14." Unpublished paper, Southern Baptist Theological Seminary, 1960.

Swank, J. Grant. "A Plea to Some Who Speak in Tongues," *Christianity Today*, 19 (February 28, 1975): 12-13.

Sweet, J. P. M. "A Sign for Unbelievers: Paul's Attitude to Glossolalia," *New Testament Studies*, 13 (April 1967): 240-57.

Swete, H. B. "Holy Spirit," *A Dictionary of the Bible*, James Hastings, editor. Charles Scribner's Sons, 1902. 2:402-11.

Talbert, Charles H. *Literary Patterns, Theological Themes and the Genre of Luke-Acts*. Scholars Press, 1974.

_____. *Luke-Acts: New Perspectives from the Society of Biblical Literature*. Crossroads, 1984.

_____. *Perspectives on Luke-Acts*. National Association of Baptist Professors of Religion, 1978.

"Taming the Tongues," *Time*, 84 (July 10, 1964): 64-66.

Taylor, R. O. P. "The Tongues at Pentecost," *Expository Times*, 40 (1928-29): 300-303.

Taylor, Vincent. *Behind the Third Gospel*. Clarendon Press, 1926.

_____. *The Gospel According to St. Mark*. Macmillan and Company, 1957.

Thackeray, H. St. J. (trans.). *Josephus*. "The Loeb Classical Library." 8 vols. William Heinemann, 1930-1938.

Thayer, Joseph Henry. *A Greek-English Lexicon of the New Testament*. 4th. ed. T. & T. Clark, 1901.

Thiselton, A. C. "The 'Interpretation' of Tongues: A New Suggestion in the Light of Greek Usage in Philo and Josephus," *Journal of Theological Studies*, 30:1 (1979): 15-36.

Thomas, K. "Speaking in Tongues." Unpublished paper, Berlin Suicide Prevention Center, 1965.

Thomas, Robert L. "The Holy Spirit and Tongues," *The King's Business*, 54 (May 1963): 9-11.

_____. "Tongues Will Cease," *Journal of the Evangelical Theological Society*, 17:2 (1974): 81-89.

Thomas, W. H. Griffith. *The Holy Spirit and Modern Thought*. Eerdmans, 1955.

Thomson, W. S. "Tongues at Pentecost: Acts 2," *Expository Times*, 38 (1926): 284-86.

"Tongues, Gift of," *Encyclopedia Britannica*. 23 vols. William Benton, 1962. 22:288-89.

Torrey, C. C. *The Composition and Date of Acts*. Harvard University Press, 1916.

Toussaint, Stanley D. "First Corinthians Thirteen and the Tongues Question," *Bibliotheca Sacra*, 120 (October-December 1963): 311-16.

Truluck, Rembert. "A Study of the Relationships Between Hellenistic Religious Ecstasy and Corinthian Glossolalia." Unpublished seminar paper, Southern Baptist Theological Seminary, 1965.

Tugwell, Simon. "The Gift of Tongues in the New Testament," *Expository Times*, 84 (February 1973): 137-40.

Tuland, Carl G. "The Confusion About Tongues," *Christianity Today*, 13 (December 6, 1968): 207-209.

Unger, Merrill F. *New Testament Teaching on Tongues*. Kregel Publications, 1971.

van Unnik, W. C. "Luke-Acts, A Storm Center in Contemporary Scholarship," *Studies in Luke-Acts*, Leander E. Keck and J. Louis Martyn, editors. Abingdon Press, 1966. Pp. 15-32.

Vivier, Lincoln Morse. "Glossolalia." Unpublished doctor's dissertation, University of Witwatersrand, 1960.

_____. "The Glossolalic and His Personality," in *Beiträge zur Ekstase*, T. H. Spoerri, editor. Basel, 1968.

Volz, Paul. *Der Geist Gottes*. J. C. B. Mohr, 1910.

Wagner, C. P. "What About Tongue Speaking?" *Eternity*, 19 (March 1968): 24-26.

Walker, Dawson. *The Gift of Tongues and Other Essays*. T. & T. Clark, 1906.

Walters, Stanley D. "Speaking in Tongues," *Youth in Action* (May 1964): 8-11, 28.

Walvoord, John F. "Contemporary Issues in the Doctrines of the Holy Spirit, Part IV: Spiritual Gifts Today," *Bibliotheca Sacra*, 130-520 (1973): 315-28.

Ward, Wayne E. "The Significance of Glossolalia for the Church," in *Speaking in Tongues: Let's Talk about It*, Watson E. Mills, editor. Word Books, 1973. Pp. 143-51.

_____. "Various Views of Tongue Speaking," in *Tongues*, Luther B. Dyer, editor. LeRoi Publishers, 1971. Pp. 9-23.

de Weale, Ferdinand J. "The Roman Meat Market North of the Temple at Corinth," *American Journal of Archaeology*, 36 (1930): 432-54.

Webster, Douglas. *Pentecostalism and Speaking With Tongues*. Highway Press, 1964.

Wedderburn, A. J. M. "Romans 8:26—Towards a Theology of Glossolalia?" *Scottish Journal of Theology*, 28:4 (1975): 369-77.

"Weeks, Feast of," *The Westminster Dictionary of the Bible*, James Hastings, editor. Westminster Press, 1944.

Weinel, Heinrich. *Die Wirkungen des Geistes und der Geister im nachapostolischen Zeitalter bis auf Irenäus*. J. C. B. Mohr, 1899.

Weiss, D. Bernhard. *Einleitung in das Neue Testament*. Wilhelm Hertz, 1886.

Welliver, Kenneth Bruce. "Pentecost and the Early Church." Unpublished doctor's dissertation, Yale University, 1961.

Welmers, William E. "Glossolalia," *Christianity Today*, 7 (November 8, 1963): 19-20.

Westwood, Tom. "Speaking in Unknown Tongues," *Bible Treasury Notes*, 6 (May 1949): 3-5.

Whitley, O. R. "When You Speak in Tongues: Some Reflections on the Contemporary Search for Ecstasy," *Encounter*, 35 (Spring 1974): 81-94.

Willet, H. L. "Question Box: New Testament References to Glossolalia or Speaking in Other Tongues," *Christian Century*, 54 (March 24, 1937): 389.

Williams, Cyril G. "Ecstaticism in Hebrew Prophecy and Christian Glossolalia," *Studies in Religion*, 3:4 (1973-1974): 320-38.

_____. "Glossolalia as a Religious Phenomenon: 'Tongues' at Corinth and Pentecost," *Religion*, 5 (Spring 1975): 16-32.

_____. *Tongues of the Spirit: A Study of Pentecostal Glossolalia and Related Phenomena*. University of Wales Press, 1981.

Williams, George H. and Edith Waldrogel. "A History of Speaking in Tongues and Related Gifts," in *The Charismatic Movement*, Michael Hamilton, editor. Eerdmans, 1975. Pp. 61-113.

Willis, Lewis J. "Glossolalia in Perspective," in *The Glossolalia Phenomenon*, Wade H. Horton, editor. Pathway Press, 1966. Pp. 247-84.

Willoughby, Harold R. *Pagan Regeneration: A Study of Mystery Initiations in the Graeco-Roman World*. University of Chicago Press, 1929.

Winn, Albert Curry. "*Pneuma* and *Kerygma*: A New Approach to the New Testament Doctrine of the Holy Spirit." Unpublished doctor's dissertation, Union Theological Seminary, 1956.

Wolfram, Walter Andrew. "The Sociolinguistics of Glossolalia." Unpublished master's thesis, Hartford Seminary, 1966.

Wood, I. F. *The Spirit of God in Biblical Literature*. A. C. Armstrong and Son, 1904.

Woolsey, Warren. "Speaking in Tongues: A Biblical, Theological and Practical Study." Mimeographed paper, Houghton, NY. Houghton Wesleyan Church, 1971.

Wright, Arthur. "The Gift of Tongues: A New View," *Theological Monthly*, 5 (1891): 161-69, 272-80.

_____. *Some New Testament Problems*. Methuen and Company, 1898.

Wright, G. Ernest. *Biblical Archaeology*. Westminster Press, 1960.

Zaugg, Elmer H. *A Genetic Study of the Spirit Phenomena in the New Testament*. University of Chicago Press, 1917.

Zeller, George W. *God's Gift of Tongues: The Nature, Purpose and Duration of Tongues as Taught in the Bible*. Loizeaux Brothers, 1978.

Zeus, Jon. "An Appraisal of the Charismatic Movement," *Baptist Reformation Review*, 11:2 (1982): 43-47.

Zimmerman, Charles. "The Gift of Tongues in 1 Corinthians." Un-
    published paper, Grace Theological Seminary, n.d.

Zohiates, Spiros. *Speaking with Tongues*. American Mission to the
    Greeks, 1964.

——————. *What the Bible Says about Tongues*. American Mission to the
    Greeks, 1964.

INDEXES

Author Index